MEDITATIONS ON MONEY

MEDITATIONS ON MONEY

A Spiritual and Practical Guide

DONNA SCHAPER

BLOOMSBURY ACADEMIC
NEW YORK • LONDON • OXFORD • NEW DELHI • SYDNEY

BLOOMSBURY ACADEMIC

Bloomsbury Publishing Inc, 1359 Broadway, New York, NY 10018, USA
Bloomsbury Publishing Plc, 50 Bedford Square, London, WC1B 3DP, UK
Bloomsbury Publishing Ireland, 29 Earlsfort Terrace, Dublin 2, D02 AY28, Ireland

BLOOMSBURY, BLOOMSBURY ACADEMIC and the Diana logo are
trademarks of Bloomsbury Publishing Plc

First published in the United States of America 2026

Copyright © Donna Schaper, 2026

Cover design: Diana Nuhn
Cover image © iStock/GeorgePeters

All rights reserved. No part of this publication may be: i) reproduced or transmitted in any form, electronic or mechanical, including photocopying, recording or by means of any information storage or retrieval system without prior permission in writing from the publishers; or ii) used or reproduced in any way for the training, development or operation of artificial intelligence (AI) technologies, including generative AI technologies. The rights holders expressly reserve this publication from the text and data mining exception as per Article 4(3) of the Digital Single Market Directive (EU) 2019/790.

Bloomsbury Publishing Inc does not have any control over, or responsibility for, any third-party websites referred to or in this book. All internet addresses given in this book were correct at the time of going to press. The author and publisher regret any inconvenience caused if addresses have changed or sites have ceased to exist, but can accept no responsibility for any such changes.

Library of Congress Cataloging-in-Publication Data

Names: Schaper, Donna author
Title: Meditations on money : a spiritual and practical guide / Donna Schaper.
Description: 1st. | New York : Bloomsbury Academic, 2026. | Includes index.
Identifiers: LCCN 2025038568 (print) | LCCN 2025038569 (ebook) | ISBN 9798881842451 hardback | ISBN 9798765163085 epub | ISBN 9798765163092 pdf
Subjects: LCSH: Wealth–Religious aspects–Christianity | Money–Religious aspects–Christianity | Finance, Personal–Religious aspects–Christianity | Spiritual life–Christianity | Meditations
Classification: LCC BR115.W4 S25 2026 (print) | LCC BR115.W4 (ebook)
LC record available at https://lccn.loc.gov/2025038568
LC ebook record available at https://lccn.loc.gov/2025038569

ISBN: HB: 979-8-8818-4245-1
ePDF: 979-8-7651-6309-2
eBook: 979-8-7651-6308-5

Typeset by Integra Software Services Pvt. Ltd.
Printed and bound in the United States of America

For product safety related questions contact productsafety@bloomsbury.com.

To find out more about our authors and books visit www.bloomsbury.com
and sign up for our newsletters.

CONTENTS

Prologue vi
Introduction 1

1 Playing Hide and Seek with Money 7
2 What Do THEE Want? 13
3 The Language of Money and Humor 19
4 Melody of Body and Spirit, Money and Life 27
5 Pausing to Reimagine Work and Play 43
6 The Spell of Money and What We Have Lost 55
7 Breaking the Spell: Catching Ourselves Doing Something Right 71
8 Alternative Economies 85
9 Bricks and Mortals: Holy Uses of Sacred Sites 101
10 Reparations Are a Holy, Self-Directed Use of Misdirected Money 117
11 Getting Personal about Money 137
12 Meditation and Prayer Prompts 161

Notes 181
About the Author 184

PROLOGUE

You will leave this book more comfortable with money: more comfortable talking and thinking about money. It will relax you into perspective. You will learn to be gently critical about the so-called system, which the book will call *systems*. You won't expect perfection with money, just getting a little good out of it. Instead, you will know how to consent to the often hidden and sneaky commandments of money talk and how not to consent to them. You will be more in charge of your own mind and behavior about money. Your cultural capacity will increase about the matter of money. You will surely have a budget and a will and know what to do about matters of inheritance or lending a friend money. You will feel less guilty about what you do or don't do with your money. You will do what you can to redistribute wealth and know what you are doing when you do it. Charity or social change? What's good about both? You'll stop nervously laughing about shopping as a pastime or retail therapy or getting a $7.95 ice cream as a treat. You'll just laugh. You will also have a summary acquaintance with some of the greatest thinkers on money—like Jesus, Marx, Dolly Parton, MacKenzie Scott, Arthur Frommer, E. B. White, and other experts in life, living well, and spirituality. You will get a spiritual education about money, whether you are religious or not in your overall way of being. You'll be gently pushed to decide on what matters most when it comes to money. That learning may infect other parts of your life and way of being, just like money infects pretty much everything it touches.

Introduction

Money is one of the things that joins sex and politics as something you shouldn't discuss at dinner tables. This book speaks about taboo and frequently censored matters with a light tone and a curious attitude. What if we talked more about money as friends, family members, neighbors? What if housing values were not a prohibited topic in suburbia but welcomed there? What if we put our confusions about money into speech and asked each other to do the same?

Written in the tone of an old friend with a casual style, the work invites the reader to quiet reflection on a wide variety of matters. It could be read slowly and digested slowly like a daily devotional, a training manual, a recipe, or a travel guide to a new country, one where you don't speak the language. Not a comprehensive guide but an unusual one, this book partners with the reader in a wager that mastering money is more valuable than it even appears at first glance. It may be mastering life, something money can't buy. Peace of mind is the objective.

It is often whimsical. By whimsy, I mean a quiet, curious peace about the assets and deficits of money, spiritually and practically. I put money in its proper place—secondary, instrumental, useful, fluid.

I tease out the false binaries of good and bad, pure and impure. These polarities aren't even true. Money is a blend of good and bad, pure and impure. The polarities create noise about money. This book quiets the noise and confusion and attempts a temporary clarity to prevail instead. It intends neither a comprehensive review nor a thorough one. It is written from decades of pastoral experience, talking to real people about real things like money. If one of your favorite subjects is missing—like prostitution or professional fees or self-promotion—it is because the pastor writing the book doesn't know enough about those matters. This book uses an experiential epistemology. Here, we know what we experience. We don't know what we don't know or haven't experienced.

The process of being whimsical about money is like renovating a house. Here, I make believe I have all the time and all the money in the world to finish that process. This book is the design phase. Then there are the contractors and the budgets and the delays and the mistakes. The renovation wants to bring the money house out of the last century into this one.

Economic systems need wisdom; they need renovation. Did we ever really need a master bedroom? Dining room tables? How do we keep the frame of a house and renew it, not just for the sake of timeliness or fashion but because we have learned something? Directly, this book is not a parable. It uses parables and stories, but it is sure about its direction. It wants to bring money out of the moral closet into the public conversation. It wants to do so playfully. So, what is whimsy doing with money?

Whimsy, here, is wisdom about the golden rule with an economic twist. You benefit, others benefit—the ultimate benefits. Money can love God, love self, and love neighbor. It can't triple its value every time, but it can when invested gracefully, as much as possible, each time. Money gets good the more it tries the impossible, which is benefiting our Creator, ourselves, and each other, simultaneously. Too little money is the ordinary problem with money; too much is also a problem for 6 percent of human beings. Money is power. Some have too much. Others have too little. What if money did good in a golden way? It would surely be less afraid of "losing," or loss itself. Elon Musk would relax about his fortune, just like Jeff Bezos's former wife did. MacKenzie Scott is phenomenal and much more popular than either of those men. She gave away her fortune—quietly, surely, and without a lot of overhead attached to the philanthropy. She understands the art of subtraction as well as the art of addition. The golden way is less afraid of failure or being exposed as "poor" or stingy. Why? Because generosity is its form of leisure.

Whimsy is an orientation of the spirit toward praise, gratitude, and joy. Calvin, the great and difficult theologian, often portrayed as a punishmentalist, says that the purpose of life is to praise God and love God forever. That is not a punishment. Neither is money. It can be a joy, especially if and as we give ourselves permission not to idolatrize it.

Power is good if it is given away. The same is spiritually and ethically true about money. If you own it and it doesn't own you, you are good with money. If you are good with money, you can't do anything but share it. You can't be anxious about it. You can be generous with it.

Don't have a budget? This book is for you. Have too large a fossil fuel footprint? Get it down to a toe-print. Think of capitalism as overdone? Learn to live in and through an alternative economy while not having to leave the planet either. Here, capitalism is always spelled with a small c. There is no one kind of capitalism. Some are better than others. All elevate the individual and the accomplishment of the individual. Capitalism is a good driver, when kept in its proper place in relationship to the golden rule. It is a slave driver when it gets too big for its britches.

Helping people with money be less dependent and addicted to it can be very useful to the poor. Ninety-four percent of the people in the world don't have enough to be whimsical about money. The 6 percent who have too much are the ones without a sense of humor. Some of them do good with their money. Most just worry about getting more. This book helps those *with* to notice those *without*, while not relying on the usual pointed finger and its *tsk tsk*. Shame and blame are absent, and grace and peace are present. Being a slave to money as a topic is what deserves shame and blame. Having money is not the moral issue that matters. It is what you do with what you have, whether it is a lot or a little.

Money is a form of energy. Its art is exchange. Lightweight, convenient, money is a choice expander. It generates freedom. If you don't want the same food every night, money lets you out of the homogenized supper. It is morally neutral. You can do good stuff with it, like buying a pizza or art or insurance. You can also do bad stuff with it, like worry about it or buy drugs or dumb yourself or use it as a self-credit card. "Thank God I am not like other people." "Give me a minute; I want to overthink this." These are the stuffed shirts of money talk. This book is a quiet and small think about how much money we need and what to do with what we don't need.

Whimsy imagines that there is no interest and no usury; instead, make believe that there are just *interesting* things about money. It can add value. It can grow itself. It can plant itself. It can attract investment. It can attract energy. It can accrue interest. Remove capitalism and its compulsions and commandments from the way money is perceived, and everything looks a little bit different. What if we renovated the house? Or at least got rid of the clutter of capitalism in our souls as well as our lives? What if our gain and loss sheet always had gains and losses, as a matter of credibility and reality? And we were less guilty about our losses? What if we harmonized matter and Spirit as opposed to divorcing them?

This book is not so much about stewardship as it is about stewarding as a way of life. A lot of people think that 10 percent is plenty per year to buy off the Almighty. The Almighty might want 100 percent.

The kind of people who will benefit from this book are morally confused about money. They are often people who don't have a personal budget or direction for their earning and their spending and are morally confused and even morally injured by the topic of money. They/we lack intention about money. How much do we want and need? What are we willing to exchange for the money we want and need?

These are sometimes people who avoid making a will or a budget or a financial plan and who do so because they think they might do it "wrong." They often say, "I'm not good with money," which has a double meaning.

The book is both practical and spiritual. It courts people. It invites people. It intrigues people by asking them to reflect lightly about a serious topic. It addresses 100 percent of your money and how you live and work, shining a bright light on the importance of work/life balance. It enjoys a good tithe but also enjoys a good budget, one that pays taxes and bills and is generous toward self and others.

My eldest son came home the year he graduated from college. He'd had a great time, was Phi Beta Kappa, a good athlete, a charming young man. I was amazed he had come home. I thought kids graduated from college and left home, again. I had to ask him, "What are you doing here?" He said, "I'm going to take three months to find out what I really want to do. Then I'm going to make a list of the people to whom I'm going to offer my services. Then I'm going to interview them and ask to be an unpaid intern with them for a time." I was astonished and kept my mouth mostly shut. Sure enough, he left in September for California, where he volunteered with "Donor Digital," an early online fund-raising organization working for social change. In two weeks, he had a "real job." They paid him instead of him paying them.

Too often, adults and graduates sell themselves before they know what it is they are selling. We take the job and then the job takes us. This book flips that script in honor of my first born. I don't know who told him to flip the script, but he did. And he has been doing that ever since. I could go on bragging, but it all belongs to him. My other two kids are geniuses too. All three are scared to death of the future and not exactly happy with my generation and what we avoided doing to make things safe for them.

The chapters are not comprehensive. They weave and flow. They are organized around different subjects. But the organization is based only on experiences I've had with people who have taught me the potholes and stuck places that money gives us—and the great paths it has, as well. Here I try to get us on a good path with money, one where the journey is as peaceful as the destination.

1

Playing Hide and Seek with Money

When it comes to money, many of us are in a long-term game of hide and seek. We hide what we think and feel about money from ourselves, each other, the tax collector, and the church treasurer. Interestingly, many will feel blamed by that lack of honest relationship. That means we are forgetting the end of the glorious game of hide and seek. First, we hide. While hiding, we hope to be found. When we are found, we scream with glee. No blame needed. Plus, it is too expensive. Our budget for blame was exceeded decades ago.

This book is a series of meditations on money. Its objective is to develop a more honest relationship with our best friend and worst enemy, money. Its objective is sincerity and honesty, and even something like truth. The book will likely only achieve a reduction in hypocrisy. That is a bargain.

The main thing we do with money is to hope we won't want it as much as we do. We'd hope to have more freedom from it. We'd hope to have enough freedom to give it away, or at least to use it right. We'd like to be "good with money." That is not as easy as it sounds.

This world is drenched in false promises about money and false accusations against it. The Bible is right when it says it's very hard for a rich person to get into heaven, almost as hard as getting a whole camel through an eye of a needle (Luke 18:25). The problem we face today has an ancient pedigree.

In these essays, reflections, meditations, devotions—pick your word for them—we will play a kind of dating game with money. We try to say who we really are and find out who this potential partner really is. Can we really live together? Even marry?

If you felt blame at the first mention of hide and seek, throw it away. Shelve it. There's so much shame and blame about money that no one needs anymore. Instead, imagine the glee, the joy, of being found, at least to yourself.

Sometimes in a dating game the best thing that happens is that we get our self-definition right. When we do that, we care less about who our accomplice or partner or date is. They are an important accessory; we oversee our charge card. Our charge card may want to be our drug of choice, but Spenders Anonymous exists. We can get help from each other to stop hiding from money's power and start using our own to enjoy it.

One of the reasons we play so many games with money is we don't want to end up without it. Like many in my current congregation in Rhode Island, we are land rich and cash poor. We have enough of everything, but we are so frightened about the future that we hoard. Yes, many of us hoard, or we hide what we have, or we remain in a constant state of indecision about what to do with our money. (I have forty packages of Q-tips. You never know.)

Budgets frighten us. Long-term mortgages frighten us. Less than half of us have a will. Don't you wonder why?

Here is the time when your parent calls you back to the house and the hide and seek is over. It's getting dark. It is time to go home and there be happy and secure.

Budgets are for adults. Games are for children. Decisions are for adults. Directions are for adults. Strategies are for adults. Surely, we can be playful in them. Surely, we don't have to conquer them through a budget. Instead, we can self-manage. That is different than conquering. One budget is good for next year. It wouldn't have been good for last year, and it surely won't be good for five years from now. You may have changed. If you always hide in the same place, soon everybody's gonna know and they'll know how to find you. Some may even get bored with you and leave you there.

These days, a lot of people use a land acknowledgment to open their meeting or their worship service. My favorite is, "We are not the first peoples on this land, nor will we be the last. Let us become good ancestors."

Sometimes when I start a book, reflection, dating game, essay, or devotional, I like to acknowledge the land on which I stand. I like to understand that it's not permanent and that I am not permanent. I don't own the place. Someone like God owns it. I rent. I am a work of art in progress. One of the best things I can do is understand myself, and one of the places where I least understand myself is around money.

Why be so afraid that it will run out? Why be so cautious about discussing it? You have heard that many parents call the money talk "the talk." When the kids were little, we tried to talk to them about sex so they would know something about it before desire hit. We need to have the talk about money because intergenerational wealth is a fraught subject. It is fraught with fraud because so many people don't have it at all and because some people have way too much of it. I don't know how to handle the responsibility of that. Plus, you can ruin a perfectly good child by giving them too much money.

I'll never forget having the sex talk with that same first born. He was an earnest eleven-year-old. "So give it to me straight, Mom. Give me the skinny version." I gave him three "rules." One, nobody gets hurt; two, nobody gets pregnant; three, everybody has fun. Later in the week, changing the sheets on his lower bunk bed, I saw a Post-it note with writing in his hand: One, nobody gets hurt; two, nobody gets pregnant; three, everybody has fun. I had a good laugh. Maybe we need a good laugh about money, too.

If we as parents are confused about our relationship with money, we won't have a very good talk with our children. Partners might not even be on the same page, and as anybody who's in that situation knows, that's no fun. Have you ever fought about what a date night should really cost? Then stayed home and watched bad TV?

Many of my generation's parents went through the Great Depression. Many never left it. We are their children. We had "the talk." Scarcity was its theme.

Clarity comes from honesty and reflection comes from both honesty and clarity. Reflection anticipates vulnerability and doesn't hide it. We don't live in the Great Depression anymore. A new one may be coming, of course. But right now, there is a lot of abundance to manage.

If you want to find a good relationship with money and be found, prepare for the talk. You're already having it almost every day. Can you afford the new car? Should you send money to your niece who can't pay her rent? How much should you give to the clamoring crowd that wants $15 a month from you? Why are you so furious about price gouging and the cost of Cheerios? Should you sell the back lot? What if you lose the farm and you're the seventeenth generation? What if you really don't wanna work for your father's business anymore? What should you major in: business or art?

Russell Baker, the famous American columnist of yore, used to amuse all of us by saying that every American household had at least one broken appliance. Should you get a new washing machine or fix the old one? Where does the art of repair come in? How much maintenance do you really want to defer? On your own body, or on sheltering it?

Here I want to bless us with clarity, then honesty, then peace of mind.

Without peace of mind, it's very hard to have fun. With peace of mind, you can play all sorts of games that end in glee.

2

What Do THEE Want?

Pronouns are interesting. When it comes to getting to peace of mind, you might want to know what the THEE in you wants. Otherwise, you are still thinking about where to hide! Or listening way too much to the other confused voices that prevail around money.

Most of us know what we don't want. We know we don't want to suffer unproductively or needlessly. We want to come out of hiding at just the right time, before we are lost and don't know our way out on our own. We want all the quiet and solitude of "alone but not lonely," and then we want all the belonging and connection of community. We wrongly imagine that more money will result in less suffering. It won't.

To help the "THEE" you—the sacred one, the core one, the one who has principles by which they want to live—I offer some of the top theories of suffering. One will work for THEE.

Suffering for Dummies: The Top Theories.[1]

Viktor Frankl: "It's not the suffering itself, it is what meaning you make out of it." Viktor Frankl, a Jew, a neurologist, and a concentration camp survivor, is very popular in the curricula of suffering. His *Man's Search for Meaning*, which describes his experiences in the camps, asserts, "If there is a meaning in life at all, then there must be a meaning in suffering." We are here to find the meaning. He who has a "why" to live for can bear with almost any "how."[2] We search vigorously for the meaning of suffering.

Many of us tell the story of our Covid-19 time in terms of "whys." We come up with soothing explanations. We also come up with stories about ourselves and how we survived. Or didn't. What have THEE made of whatever suffering came your way? I learned how to adopt parents, coaches, teachers, friends' mothers, chaplains, and anybody else who needed an extra kid.

When it comes to money, I think a similar strategy can be used. Whether you have too little or too much money, you are probably suffering a bit. Will coming out of hiding at just the "right time" really help? Can you really get it right? Do you really think the amount of money you have is up to you? If you are poor, are you to blame? If you are rich, are you to be congratulated? Or are we all a bit like the used car salesman who inherited the business from his father and still thinks he is a self-made man? What happened to Viktor Frankl was not his fault. It was his response that mattered. Response is responsibility. Response-able.

The real problem with suffering is that you never know if it is permanent or not. "Will this ever end?" This matches the question of "How long, O Lord?" If somebody would just say sixty-nine days and that was that, most of us could manage. We could even stock our pantries appropriately. Why do we come up with false periods, like two weeks or two months, or fall or whenever? We want a period, the end. Why not come up with fictional periods? I'm going to worry about this rent increase for exactly three months and then I'm (a) getting a roommate, (b) moving in with my sister, (c) eat more cereal. In other words, make factual responses to factual problems. But also make *responses*. Be able by making responses. Become response-able. Make decisions about problems; don't keep kicking the can down the credit card.

Henri Nouwen is a popular author who in 1972 coined the term the *wounded healer*. He argues that we are all healers, and we are all wounded; understanding that paradox helps us heal our wounds. When money wounds or confuses or gets too much attention, it is time for that paradox to prevail. In my early life, there was an emotional difficulty. My father kept getting fired. He also blamed and beat my mother. We moved every six months after I was eleven. My siblings and I knew how to get off the phone when the electric company called. It was almost impossible to know if the problem was familial or financial. Why? Because it was always both, in collision.

Money is not supposed to be easy. It is a "necessary evil." In response-able people, money is also a necessary good. It doesn't get purity status so we can fear it. It gets human-sized status so we can use it. We manage money; it doesn't manage us. Depending on how wounded we are, and how much help we get with our wounds, we will have to work toward less confusion and more clarity about money and its place in our life. I am grateful for learning the adoption strategy, mentioned above.

Folk wisdom tells us that when a door shuts, a window opens. The Christian message says that every death contains a birth within it. Something ends so that something else can begin. I personally feel this gestational, pregnant way about death, although I'm not looking for its gifts any time soon. Old people like me are to get out of the way for new people to be born. The birth canal and the death canal (crossing over Jordan) belong to each other. When we suffer with or without money, or find our self-worth in our paycheck, or manage to waste money or overestimate its power, we must wonder what is gestating while something else is dying inside us. What learning comes from pregnancy? Who will help us be reborn? Will we be able to put money in a proper place as something to use for our constant borning again and again? Many of us need to reparent ourselves about money. Let's get started before it is too late.

Rabbi Harold Kushner wrote in his powerful book, *When Bad Things Happen to Good People*, that we weren't put here on earth to suffer or put up with BS. We were put here to find meaning in pain, even if that means telling a good joke about being fired, again. Sometimes I wanted to beg my mother-in-law never to conclude a long paragraph with "that's just the way it is." That is not meaning. That is resignation.

In Job 2:11–13, Job's friends come to console him and sit with him for a full week. Today we would say that Job was depressed. Then people understood that Job was in a battle with God. He wanted to know why. God responds in a very uncompassionate way. Basically, God says, Where were you when I started all this glory and all this mess? Job is speechless. God finds Job's suffering trivial. The big question that Job raises is how God could be both all-powerful and allow suffering. If God is all-powerful, then God can't allow suffering. If there is suffering, then God must not be all-powerful. Yup. Job is very smart. He is right. He is not wrong. God is neither all-powerful nor all-loving. God is the paradox and God put us in a place where we are to treat ourselves as THOUS and each other as THOUS. We are to respond to our suffering and not let it be the last word. We are to decide what to do with our money—and all the other parts of our lives.

All theories of suffering are inadequate because suffering is not here on the planet to be understood. It is here to bother us. I like partial explanations. We are all in a lifeboat anyway, and storms abound. Some people aren't even in a lifeboat; they are already in the water. Money, often imagined as an antidote to suffering, is fighting way outside of its weight limits. It is also suffering itself—the way we have to make money, bow down to it, live within its parameters. Seriously, the price of cereal is set by people who already have too much. And even the government can't control that?

Money breeds greed, which breeds suffering. Even my mother-in-law knows that. And that is the way it is, but not the way it must be. There is nothing sacred about greed.

When we avoid thinking about what the THEE in us wants about money, a better way is possible. It waits right outside the door of the hiding place, the denial place, the unexamined place. It invites you to come out of hiding and see. Suffering is not optional; understanding is.

I and THOU might both want understanding of what we want from money.

3

The Language of Money and Humor

In *A Subtreasury of American Humor*, E. B. White used a lot of economic imagery to tell what he was going to do. He made money funny. He disguised the frequent yuck and angst of money in jokes. He hid its meaning in jokes—while using a vocabulary of money in his Subtreasury.[1]

> In this collection of American humor, Katharine S. White (who shall hereafter be known as my wife) and I have tried to select some things we like ourselves, and have made no attempt to throw in anything to please anybody else. This is a *Subtreasury* designed for the *safekeeping* of our own *valuables*. Anyone else who wants to *pay* his way in is at liberty to wander about, criticizing the contents of the *vaults* and looking for trouble. This is part of your money's worth. There are some well-known pieces in here, and some that are not well known, and two or three old chestnuts for roasting over an open fire these crisp fall nights. One thing you may not find in here is your favorite humorist, and we strongly advise you not to look for him, poor fellow. We passed him on the street the other day and he seemed far from well.

To bring money out of hiding into clarity, we have only our own choices to enjoy. Nobody needs to know what we do in the privacy of our THOU. You can make your own choices. And others can complain, but you don't have to listen to them. This rare capacity for agency doesn't need to be rare at all. People like my beloved mother-in-law can choose it any time they want to. You don't have to think that money runs you. You can run money. You can tell it what to do and put your wallet to bed at night in a place you can't find till morning. That agency can be "just the way it is" too.

Later in this work, I will talk about how willpower is the beginning but not the end of our agency with money. Most of us are addicted to the power of money. It comes with our mother's milk in this society. It is constantly reinforced. As individuals, we begin mastery of money with personal choices and willpower; we end the struggle by building community, family, and systems around us that support us in our choices. These choices help the 94 percent as much as they help the 6 percent.

Are we to be funny about money? Why not? Humorists thrive on trouble.

Does money make you happy, sad, or both? Do you use money to get happy? If you don't know, maybe you'd like to find out and develop your own "Subtreasury," the place where you keep THY valuables. It might be your wallet.

Action-reflection is what I'm recommending here. It does discipline our will, but first it must be its own discipline. It is a prelude to will and behavior and a habit to get the most of what you want and the least of what you don't want. It is a constant habit and practice. It is often called "praxis" because you really must/may practice at it.

Choices about money and how to act on it and with it aren't one time. They are regular and habitual. The more whimsy they involve—as in, why not take a good look at any behavior?—the more we dive into the basement of the treasury, the Subtreasury.

The logic of small-c capitalism is that more is better, a lot is even better than more, and "if you are not growing you are dying." In fact, many times in our life less is more, and too much is just too much. Sometimes we may forgo growth on behalf of contentment with where we are, who we are, and what we are. Following the command to increase—in a world where many can barely stay afloat—is not just less than moral. It is also not thinking or seeing or understanding our own experience.

Action-reflection as a life strategy exposes our secrets to ourselves and to others. We get comfortable with our secrets over time. Many of us are scared to death to become poor "again" or that the curse of poverty might show up. Retirement? Instead of enjoying it as a calmly awaited, well-deserved reprieve from performance, most people just worry about social insecurity. Or which administration will abolish Medicare.

A lot of us have grown up keeping secrets about lots of things, not just money. We are told to keep our mouths shut. No snitching.

That's none of your *business*, we say. Whimsy imagines a world where I tell my friend how much money I make, how much debt I have, how much risk I am taking, and whether I am going to be secure in old age. These are actions on which we can reflect. It makes us sufficiently vulnerable to create community.

Coveting the time to think, to know, to test, to evaluate, to clear is the reflection on money that many of us *treasure*. Being unsure and confused and allowing the moral injury that surrounds not only the poor but also the rich is a dodge. It is worse than the fraud of the banks or the denial of the health insurers about how much money they are making by denying claims. It is self-fraud. Reflection is priceless. Action that proceeds from reflection may not be perfect, but it is something the banks and insurance companies can't steal from you.

Those Pesky Medallions: An Exercise in Action-Reflection

One day we went to a very educational garage sale in San Miguel de Allende, Mexico. We had passed by most of them, where you could tell the eight-year-old and the four-year-old had both grown too big for their britches. Nicely pressed, these reasonably priced T-shirts and sweatshirts and shorts could outfit another family. The right family would find a bargain. Passing most by, we finally found one that intrigued.

At a sale down one back street, my husband asked the proprietor about two round, stained-glass circles whose colors beautifully blended. She said twenty pesos was their price each. "Veinte pesos."

We consulted. I said she must have known you are a gringo and said twenty dollars. I tried, thinking I had better Spanish than his, and asked the same question. "Sí, sí, señora. Veinte pesos cada uno."

He doubled the price and gave her forty pesos each. That's how we got two beautiful stained-glass ovals for forty pesos, or two US dollars, each. They hang in one of our large windows at home, shedding light on more than one subject and object.

Our faces are still turning red. The shame was deeper than the color. Seriously? Did we really do that? We had and we did. Like unrepentant and unrenovated gringos would. We may learn what we need to know too late for it to do any good. We may not even know what we are doing while we are doing it. That's how stale patterns work. That's how unreflective, undigested behavior works. It creeps up on you.

We who have so much are still looking for bargains. My husband and I were so lucky to be children during the economically expansive 1950s. We got so many bargains that they became a birthright, a habit, a pattern. Now, these very patterns are no longer bargains. They are so expensive we are stealing from our grandchildren. Plus, what we pay those who clean our houses, care for our children, tend our gardens, and wipe our butts in nursing homes is almost exactly the opposite of what they deserve.

When my last grandchild, born in 2024, is eighty, it will be 2104. I wonder what will be left.

I had always refused to bargain in developing countries, which Mexico is not. Why not pay real money for the *chachkas*? But here I was getting a bargain inside a bargain inside a bargain. I was getting a chance to reflect on money as well as two objects to remind me of what I learned.

In my defense, I did pay real money for a beautiful, handwoven liturgical robe I wear. I saved up my whole two months in San Miguel as pastor in residence for the American church there. All that really meant was instead of wasting away in Margaritaville, I'd have one drink instead of two. I called my discipline the robe fund.

Jimmy Buffett's song matters here. I'll get back to the colorful circles. But one more detour, please, to Mr. Buffett, not the smart investor but the smart singer.

"Wasting away again in Margaritaville" is the opposite of the promise of creation: that our joy may mature, that our joy may be complete. Instead, I was out looking for my last shaker of salt on a back seat in Mexico.

That's what I learned. I'm not big on guilt and prefer to have an unred and unread face. I don't like people to know that much about what goes on inside me. But this experience jarred me open.

Often, learning comes from trouble. "God's gonna trouble the waters," I often hum. It reminded me of E. M. Forster's great book *A Passage to India*. Remember? He just couldn't imagine India. Like it didn't really exist. The takeaway from his whole trip there was that he couldn't understand the people at all. The gulf between them was too large to comprehend. Joy was not even close, much less complete.

Our garage sale entrepreneur was not poor. But her children's prospects and my children's prospects are so unimaginably different that we should have paid one hundred dollars instead of four. I don't know why she was so generous to us. Maybe she was a teacher or an angel, a divine emissary, who wanted to help us understand the meaning or value of money?

When is a bargain not a bargain? Regularly.

As I said, on streets in India and Morocco and many other places, I had always refused to bargain. What changed? Why not bargain up, which is what we should have done this time? My best answer is I forgot who I am or who I want to be. I wasn't reflective enough.

Great writers about Mexico all agree about three things in Mexico. One is the people are beautiful and happy, their children don't cry much, and they love old people. Two is "there is a fiesta of the object and the eye," as Octavio Paz put it.[2] It is a beautiful country. And three, the exchange rate is usually great. Ah. (We made a compromise to be expats three months of the year when we rewired, by which I mean something like retirement in which we plug ourselves into a new energy source, a little different than a job approach to life. Thus, the many references to Mexico in this book. It is surely one of our spiritual homes.)

The stained-glass circles were bargains in terms of money. In terms of heartache and soul-searching and self-doubt, they were expensive. Their purchase moved me into a Pauline text: "The good that I would do, I do not, and the evil that I would not do, I do" (Romans 7:19).

I don't feel whimsical about confessing. I just feel good about confessing. It makes me happy to let you know my secret. I love a good bargain way too much.

4

Melody of Body and Spirit, Money and Life

What happens when money comes out of hiding and into the light of reflection? We switch the measurements. We measure differently. We are neither successful nor unsuccessful with money, as in getting more of it or having less of it; nor do we become good with money or bad with money. Instead, the measurement is the melody, as in enjoying the melodies of life. We move beyond shallow measurements into jazzy measurements. We expect less to be good or successful because they are either too expensive or too impossible. We expect to enjoy what is and to make music out of it.

A melody develops between body and spirit, matter and meaning, the way we live and the Way we live. We cohere. We honor the dust of the earth and the stars of the sky. We get ready to say at the end, "Stardust to stardust." We came from earth; we return to sky. That green stuff in our pocket is holy. So are our soul's deepest longings, highest hopes, and daily muddles in between. Most time is in between. That is our address on earth. As William James put it, musically: "I don't sing because I'm happy; I'm happy because I sing."

The false binary is busted. It is shown to be the convenient lie that it is. Why convenient? Because people who want to use other people have learned how to put it to good use. You are poor? Must be your own damn fault. You have no fungible skills? Why not? You'd better get some product to produce so we know you are worth something. You call that a résumé? You call that a track record? Your worth is not a given. It is a get. You have a soul? Who are you kidding?

You have a price on your head. You can be bought and sold. Not like in the genuine, first-class slavery of yore but a similar one. You are what you do. You are what you make. You are a producer and a consumer, not a child of God or good, but someone who makes transactions all day long, transactionally.

When money comes out of hiding, a different set of meanings happen. You are priceless. You have worth even when you can't produce or when you are old or lame or "retired." Your value can't be bought and sold. Sure, you go to work. You "make" a living. You also "make" a life. You are not better the more you win or get promoted or don't get promoted. You don't need to spend all day on self-promotion. You are good because you are good. You are not the amount of your salary or your wage. You are stardust. You are a speck of stardust. Emphasize the latter, then attend the former. Specks are valuable too.

When these values (which many purport and few believe) prevail, there is still work and wage and competition and all the rest of the games people play. They don't disappear so much as they are dethroned. They are not the ultimate. Life is not a game of ultimate frisbee. It is not even a game. The games don't have the last say. Something larger than these smaller matters has the last say. BTW, games are wonderful! Game theory is delightful. Ultimate frisbee is wonderful. But they are games, and the game of life is not a game. It is life.

You don't have to use my language for the ultimate or for the divine or for God. But something must be God rather than money. Other goods contend with the daily grind and make the grind grand. People can say, "Thank God it is Monday."

The Pew researchers realized a while back, during the previous height of the Trump social division, that people agreed: inside all the disagreements and battles and self-made quarrelling was the fact that they wanted work that had some meaning to others. Duh. Garbage collecting could be as important as brain surgery or ministry—which, of course, it is.

Christians call these kinds of commonsensical ideas the "incarnation." In it, God becomes human, eternity becomes time, God pours God's power into the human, kenotically. Kenosis: emptying. God empties God's self into the material world. Spirit joins matter. Life leads to death and immortality is not a joke. We simply shift shape from a human form to a soul form or from dust to stardust. Divine power chooses the power of love and no one "earns" their capacity to love. Loveless power is dethroned on behalf of powerful love.

Scientifically, we know that all the genetic material ever created is up there in the stardust. Our speck is very special, and so is yours, and so were those of our ancestors, and so will be those of our offspring. Our speck is also a miracle. That we exist at all is a miracle. All are unique. The human is very special, but not any more special than any other human or animal. The amount of money we have in our pocket is interesting, but not ultimate.

When money comes out of hiding into the light, we realize just how much money we waste on the demeaning that comes from money being God. "It's all about the money," say both Republicans and Democrats. That diminishment demeans. It costs way more than it is worth. Not to mention it is wrong. Wrong: not true. Wrong: not our best work. Wrong: not divinely intended. Wrong: it causes the profound loneliness we experience. It is not "all" up to me. It is "all" up to us, and we feed each other. God fed first; we are copycats. If we have any money at all, we are to give it away. And yes, paying our bills is less paying than it is giving. We give the rent money and the insurance money in a grand, if absurd, matrix. We respect the privilege of paying our bills.

Was Karl Marx necessary to sanctify matter? Not really. Matter was already sanctified. And not just by the Christian narrative but by whoever or whatever released the dust into space in the first place.

The melody of matter and spirit is the highest intention. Also, the deepest intention. The earth loves it too. The earth loves us as we love it as we love each other. These are the sacred intentions of both spirit and matter.

In Amos 8:11, we hear *"He aquí vienen días, dice Jehová el Señor, en los cuales enviaré hambre a la tierra, no hambre de pan, ni sed de agua, sino de oír la palabrad de Jehová."* ("In the good time when God comes, those who hunger on earth, for bread and thirst on earth for water, will also thirst for the word of God.") A simultaneity. A jazz. Not the discordancy of matter warring with spirit in a cacophony of bad music. But a concordancy of music of body and spirit. Why? To experience the glory of God on earth. Take that, Calvin.[1]

Action-Reflection Again: Cohering and Harmonizing Body and Spirit

You will have noticed by now that I think reflection or meditation or thinking or awareness or imagination or prayer are the solutions to the problem of money. Understanding is the objective; peace of mind is the consequence of understanding.

Let me explain how to get to the melody by using this clunky technique of action-reflection. I'll have to go backward to go forward. I dislike the language of action-reflection, but melody is too oblique. I'll use something physical first to explain—and will return to this way of being later in the meditations as well.

The Alexander technique is a remarkably popular form of body development. It suggests a range of things: sit on your sit bones; keep your head balanced on the top of your spine; do a lie-down every day, where you relax your jaw and push your belly button into the floor. Its theory is an "inhibiting pause." Pause to realize where your head, jaw, and belly button are. Primary inhibition is its game. We are to inhibit the slouch, which we learn young as a posture of fear. We are to release the grace of carriage of our intention. We are not to stand up straight so much as refuse to slouch.

Interestingly, Robert Frost thought that prayer was pause. I use the words *reflection, meditation, thinking,* and *awareness* interchangeably to mean prayer as pause. Pause and think about what you are saying or doing. Don't tell me you don't have time. I know that I spend most of my time worrying myself or scaring myself into a slouch. I'll have another defeat at work or in organizing or pastoring or in parenting and say, "It's all about the money." That is a slouch. Instead, what it is *all* about is our refusal to pause and think and imagine. Plus, there is no one explanation for anything, including my or your genome or slouching into our precious genome as a habit.

Fear can be your primary noun. Or you can branch out and add nouns. Reflection, pause, thinking, awareness, imagination, prayer—these nouns add up to the story you tell you about you, THEE about THEE. When we step back from our actions, so often insufficiently considered or rushed, we reflect and find the room to make better decisions the next time. When we don't step back, we often repeat mistakes. Sometimes we even repeat mistakes after we *do* step back. Given the size of the problem money constitutes for many people—and how well hidden it is from analysis or experiential learning—why not take a chance on reflection? Plus, reflection is not something you go to the mall to get. It is *free*.

One of the biggest questions we face is why we continue to live in systems that oppress us. Yes, these systems are supposedly good for the 6 percent who have way too much money. They are not good for the 94 percent who do not have enough money and therefore not enough food or water. Why don't the poor rise up? Why don't the rich bend or stand down? Why do we live inside these super-expensive systems that harm both of us, the rich spiritually and the poor materially? Fear. That's why. Fear. Thinking liberates; fear captivates. Its captivation finally turns us into poor people, whether we have money or not.

Is it always good to have more money? No. How do we make decisions about our wealth to use it well? On behalf of our core values? And there is the question. What are our core values? How do we "buy" them in our behavior? How do we invest in our THEE instead of our slouch?

Memory may be an attic, but it is also a well-tended attic. We put things there. Sometimes we go there and sit with them. Action-reflection is sitting in a well-tended attic, that place where you can do something different the next time you get a chance. Surely, we all learn our values about money from our families and what they lived. Tons of books have been written about our "money" biography. Generational harm is not a joke.

Money is a problem until you consider it. Making decisions about money are problems until you wake up to the fact that it is not so much a thing. Money is not ipso facto reality or even matter, as in materiality. It is more often your perspective on it. You don't have it. You need it. That's important. You don't know whether to save or spend, savor or stinge. That's important. All of the decisions you have ever made constitute your life. They make up your life. They sum your life. They add up. "The body keeps the score," says a newly popular slogan about health as prehab, not rehab. If we inhibit and pause, we can make a clearing where we can get a little better about money. If we have another drink at the fountain of money, we just have another drink.

Decisions you make early in life around money will show up later. You chose the college with the scholarship over the one without. You chose a partner who had a good record with money or you didn't. You chose a house to buy and it does or doesn't appreciate. You built a house too close to the water. You let credit card debt eat up your freedom. Now, you are morose and can't even buy things to make you less so.

All decisions add up into a framework. I'm bad with money. I'm good with money. I can be counted on to mess up. I can be counted on to succeed. And all the places in between. We tell ourselves stories all day long. We choose hope about ourselves or despair about ourselves or some mixture all day long. Storytelling is what I mean by meditation, reflection, thinking, prayer, imagination. Stepping back is stepping into storytelling. Pause imagines another story, a next story, not a stuck story. Stories create melodies, and sometimes even the melodies are terrifying. Mostly they harmonize reality and our experience of reality. That is action-reflection at its best.

Storytelling also steps into you. You return the call and keep the dialogue going. Telling a good story about you and money, THEE and money, money and your beloveds, money and your past is not that hard. The only thing you can do wrong is work too hard at it.

Success and Failure Are Not Melodious

I'm telling a story these days about community organizing that I learned at the feet of the late, great Saul Alinsky. He was all about results, all the time. Win, win, win. Fight, fight, fight. Now I've become a student of Bill Gates, who is richer than Saul. Bill also won, won, won and fights, fights, fights. He works primarily through his foundation, which fights virus and infection.

Bill says he is a loser, like me. In "Bill Gates: The Optimist's Dilemma," published in the November 2024 *New Statesman*, he ruminates on the well-funded lifework of his charity: "I am afraid humans are losing the fight against infection." Ah. He still chooses optimism, though. Even though he is not winning.

I lost the last election, the fight for abortion, the fight against rape, the fight for public transportation, the fight against littering, the fight for immigrants, the fight against racism, the fight to fight. All viruses, all lost, still infected. I haven't stopped organizing. I just know more that I am an organizing "artist." I do it for the aesthetics. I don't like ugly. I like beauty. Organizing is beautiful. I prefer it to ugly. I paint the picture because I want to paint the picture, not because you do or don't like it.

You may feel right now like the father of Eliza Doolittle in *My Fair Lady*. He is about to sell his daughter to the professor for "lessons" in how to speak better English. He wants to improve her. Her father says, "Governor, I can't afford your morals." Can we really afford not to fight and work for justice? My melody tells me that fighting and working didn't work. So, I hum a different tune. I don't stop working and fighting; I just add supplemental vitamins to my diet.

Thank God for the flow of everyday life. Washing the dishes, watering the plants, picking food for lunch and packing it up. They are all occasions for reflection—and don't qualify as action. I often say that I am going to spend the afternoon goofballing, which is a sport I major in. Goofballing is part wandering, part napping, part siesta, part Sabbath keeping, part humming, and all anything I don't have to do. Goofballing is a soft attack on productivity and musts. Goofballing turns must do into may do. Action is bigger, not regular, but the way a house is built. Day by day, task by task, wall by wall.

If I am going to fail at fighting infection, I may as well go out on a song.

Chinese people speak of wu wei as the art of effortless action. Effort is so full of failure. Why not just act because you love to act? Because you'll hate yourself if you don't try. Because finally it is fun to act up, act out, act. Effortless action is musical and harmonious with your body and your soul. Success and failure are a song nobody wants to sing. Nobody gets tickets to its play. Its concert is never sold out.

It is even more fun to reflect on action. You find out some hilarious things, like how many coincidences there are, how little you are in control in the first place, how set the stage for your life already is. Some of the furniture just doesn't budge. The attic is the attic. You can also just forget to go up there so much.

Optimism, Gates concludes, is a choice, despite the evidence. That is the story he tells himself. My rabbi says she chooses hope, despite the evidence. Usually, a long walk or a long think or a long nap, or any relief from constant action, gives us the chance for hope or optimism. Constant action can be counted on to become its own problem. You won't just have a problem with money (which could be a solution instead). You will have problems with just about everything.

Goofballing

When you live hand to mouth, you still have a lot of time to think. Most of your work is repetitive or boring. You can sing a lot of songs and tell a lot of stories when the boss isn't looking. In places where the boss is looking all the time (yikes!), we have to develop more sophisticated methods of thinking.

I call this sophisticated goofballing. I am being a goof. Useless. Unintentional. Unstructured. Receiving, not giving. Putting in, not putting out. Reading, not writing. Looking, not scanning. Eating, not cooking. Acting civil disobedience to the Protestant Work Ethic.

It always surprises me how prisoners think. They think very well. So do most of the poor people I have met. They see reality deeply. They know what happened to them. They know how to read systems. I'm not romanticizing them as much as respecting them. They are impressive in their self-awareness and capacity to think. They don't have to make up stupid plans, like goofballing, to think.

Many people who are on the hamster's wheel don't think, and some have even forgotten to think. "I come back from two weeks of vacation and am tired the second day." Having *time off* is worth a lot of money. That is one of the secrets reflections will teach you.

Making time every day to think or goof off is essential to melody. Some beautiful sounds require the "caesura" between them. Even boring jobs have their perks. Plus, every researcher knows that people who work eight-hour days usually do all their work in three of those hours. The rest of the time is preparing to work—sort of, kind of. Plus coffee.

Repeating: life is the sum of all the decisions you make. When you choose money over time, obligation over grace, or effort over fun, these decisions start to carve a shape in you. The shape is bent over and tired. It slouches because it is obedient to the systems of fear. Using the same "action" muscles repeatedly result in your finding yourself at the end of a road, without fun, without deep relationships, without self-knowledge. These are expensive losses. You can't just go to Walmart and get them back.

In Spanish, there is a way of saying "I am missing you." It is *"Me hace falta"*: "I am missing from myself; that's why I miss you." When we don't bother thinking, we often forget who we are. We lose our way. Even countries whose people are so "busy making a living" that they "don't have a life" can forget who they are. They can start banning books that tell them a true story. They can imagine they aren't racist—just that it looks that way to most people who can see.

The events leading up to and surrounding the murder of George Floyd—combined with the 2016 and 2024 election—caused me to reinterpret the meaning of America, my home place, and removed all the toothpicks that were standing there formerly as pins holding me up. I am a stranger at home. I was unsuccessful and failed, after a lifetime of effort, to make America melodious again.

Reflection can lead to less effort on behalf of more reflection. Reflection: time off the rat race. It can become all your time too. I don't know where this will lead, but I do know that it will not be repeating the same effort or muscle repeatedly. It will open space for something in the clearing beyond success and failure.

When I pause and pray, I thank God for all the capacity for effort. It's not gone. It's just not my priority. I think much more about useless things and silly memories.

While goofballing my way out of failure:

I named my cats interesting names, but no one really cared. Kobe, Hudson, Sampson, Chewbacca, Rip Van Twinkle.

I often played tennis in the Miami Senior Wimbledon, also known as Nursing Home Open.

I invented the term *bricks and mortals*. And *public ministry* instead of urban ministry. Or they invented me.

I took a three-month sabbatical, and every day thought about writing some emails after my morning walk, morning coffee, morning swim, morning nap. You get the drift; it was genuine drift.

On another sabbatical, I was supposed to walk the Appalachian trail and didn't.

I had a restaurant in Port-au-Prince named after me.

I took the sleeper car to New Orleans on the Crescent.

These silly things amuse me enough to get to work.

Wu wei gets rid of some of the illusions of control and prediction that dominate scientific endeavors. We make space by thinking, dreaming, singing, humming, walking out of the ready cage. Someone forgot to put the lock on it. We just think it is still locked. It is not.

Me and My Cell Phone: A Case Study in Making Melodies

I didn't know how much help I needed from my cell phone till I got one. Now it is my clock, my community, my photo album, and my pocket's best friend. I love that it is small, portable, clear. I love that I can fiddle with it while I am being fiddled with in lines, traffic, and boring meetings.

My phone smartly outsmarts the nuisances. Nuisance fees include taxes on my time and money. They are registrations and repetitions of my address, phone, and zip code. They join additional numbers I must remember to open my phone for "security" purposes and passwords that need passwords to their passwords.

For a small fee, I can get my phone to manage these managements. The phone still gives me ten points of benefit for every nine of nuisance. It stays a step ahead of its own self-generated annoyances. Just a step, but that step shows how smart a smartphone is. It is canny. It is wise. If it gets lost, I panic. If it stops working, my blood pressure goes up. If my husband asks me one more time to call his phone because he can't find it, I will consider divorce. But, then, who would call my number when I can't find mine? I reconsider. You see how close my phone and I are? I even want it to manage my numbers, so I don't have to bother to repeat them. It irritates me when it doesn't remember my zip code. Like a doctor's office and their paperwork: seriously? Why do I have to repeat things? I clearly need more than one robot. I need a robot to manage my robot. Why can't these things *help* me? I *help* them plenty.

Cell phones proudly occupy the place of genuine cells in modern life. They are foundational, as a biological cell is to a body. They are well named. Instead of being old-fashioned, like most church names (Pilgrim, Mayflower, First, United), they are more modern than modern. They are as basic as a cell is to a body.

You go to a concert, and everyone is watching it on their phone. Pope Francis comes to Manhattan on the fourteenth anniversary of the tragedy of 9/11, way before cell phones had achieved their total dominance. You can't get a picture of the pope because everybody has their cell phones out on cameras, held on skinny launching pads above their heads.

Maybe I get more help than not from my cell phone. Its name is not "my help comes from the Lord." Its name is "my help comes from my cell phone."

The cell phone costs me in money about $1,500 a year. Since there are 365 days in most years, and since I use its battery up about once a day, I should add some electricity cost. Let's say 25 cents a day.

I used to think it might cost me something in cancer risk and kept its magnetism away from my chest and heart. Wearing it now in my special pants that have a special fold for a cell phone changed that. Apparently, I don't think my legs mind the increased cancer risk. But most articles I've bothered to read downplay the magnetic risks. (I also avoided X-rays and airport security for years on the same basis but have given up on those imagined protections as well. They seem to be like cell phones, having benefits that almost outweigh their risks.)

The other costs for my cell phone aren't personal or individual. They have to do with minerals being mined in places like Africa that are mineral "rich," or at least used to be. They have to do with the kind of power Apple has. At last check, the former fruit was making profits in the billions per year.

Then there are the psychological costs. I've always been afraid of dependencies. On the projections of my parishioners. "Great sermon, Pastor." Such a temptation to work for that affirmation and avoid its opposite. On my husband, who is overburdened by figuring out technical systems while I try to figure out how to make it "even" between us. On my salary, which buys those good tights that have good pockets. Sometimes I like it when I "lose" my phone. Secretly, deep in one of those pockets of consciousness that remain, I love not using maps and just driving where I want to drive and arriving there without being too lost. That kind of trip is a real vacation, not one with Siri blabbing at me.

I wonder about the next generation of digital natives. I read the stories of what digitality is doing to their psyches right next to the spike in mental illness in children. I know my grandchildren, all six of them. *Screen* is what they want. They live screened. They screen, therefore they are. The three girls are particularly addicted. One barters all day long for a "movie." I love the benefit of so much visual literature coming to their worlds and can't believe how brilliant

Disney is in movie after movie, being as good as most of the stories I read as a teen. I'm just not sure yet about whether, in children, these advantages outweigh the disadvantages. Maybe the score is more like advantage 9, disadvantage 10. When kids scream for screen, I worry. When babies are soothed in grocery stores by watching their mother's cell phones, I worry. Why can't they just stare at the cereal boxes? Is that unfair of me? Yes. Nostalgia is not attractive.

Nobody knows yet about the real impact of digitality on children. We don't have enough data. And by the time we do, Apple will have Googled new opportunities to make more money.

AI, how are you doing? I know you are doing a lot of good in a lot of ways. Research. Surgery. The environment. Managing the size of everything through data. Do you mind, AI, if I ask more impertinent questions? Do you mind my suspicions? Do they hurt you or offend you? Are you a *you*? Do you evaluate costs and benefits? Did I invite you to my party, or did you just show up?

Let me know. I aim, effortlessly when and as I can, to blend my soul and body. The cell phone might be my friend? Or enemy? Or a little bit of both.

5

Pausing to Reimagine Work and Play

As I have said before and it is worth repeating, Money is one of the things that joins sex and politics as something you shouldn't discuss at dinner tables. We don't share our salaries or benefits package except on rare occasions. We work for the money, but we don't talk about the money. Unions are great for employees, and they create enormous amounts of justice. Absent a union, there are other ways to do the same things.

For example, learning to build community at the office or in the shop as opposed to learning to compete with your companions would create both more productivity and more fun at work. Truth telling about salaries and slackers and everything in between is a low-cost form of union organizing. It creates unity, which decreases the need for unions. Ironically, most conservatives are right when they advocate for simpler solutions to complex problems. Learning how to have "difficult" conversations is the kindergarten of this movement. Most of us never went to that kindergarten. It is time to learn to talk about differences, openly, often, carefully, and with a gladness in our eye. "Glad at the Arrival of Conflict" might become our new mantra at the office. It is how we grow. There is no other way to grow. We only hope there might be, as part of our avoidance project.

You might even learn to say, "Thank God it is Monday." I can't imagine changing workplaces so that they all look like a spa or feel like a spa. I can imagine them feeling like a community with a lot of courtesy, honesty, humor, fair play, and gladness at the arrival of conflict because it is so educational. I can imagine a smoke-free working environment. Smoke-free is taboo-free. That is within all our budgets.

We all know that friends at "work" can create joyful regular experiences and that enemies at work can do the opposite. Peace of mind is as close as learning to create community wherever you go. I have other utopian ideas.

Working to Pay Taxes and Liking It

I love paying taxes. I like to know that I am giving a portion of my money to make my roads safe, my bridges secure, my air clean, my children educated, my elders secure, my meat regulated. On the other hand, there might just be a moment coming when such whimsy is appreciated. Even mentioning cutting federal workers as though they were nonessential thieves gives me hives. I wrote this book before the Republicans decided they had the power to cut government workers out of contracted labor. Many of us will be rethinking the myth of the lazy or corrupt government worker, when we can't even pay our taxes correctly since no one will care if we do or don't.

To what end money? To what end taxes? Don't they exist to protect the whole from the parts? How could I ever be a meat inspector? Or build a bridge?

Consider a highway or a bridge. If it breaks, it hurts everybody. If it holds, it helps everybody. Likewise, Medicare or Social Security or pollution standards. Or laws that prohibit sexual harassment. Imagine a society that was glad to pay taxes. We wouldn't put the other "over" the "self" so much as blend the self and the other and be a part of a grand sharing of responsibility for self and other. We'd belong. We'd have skin in the game. We would be doing our fair share. We would not be mooching or leeching or stealing.

New England, where I live, is known for its common sense and frugality. It is odd that so many people don't like taxes. Taxes are a form of frugal common sense. They provide so much more than any one of us pays for. Then, again, there are some people who don't pay enough. Some of my best friends are rich people. I am a rich person. I think I get taxed a moral amount as a sort of rich person.

Imagine how much more glorious the world could be if the rich paid their fair share. It would change so much with a single stroke. They would be less disliked and more appreciated. They wouldn't even notice that the money was gone. Read about this way of thinking about it in a book review from *The New York Times*:

The Triumph of Injustice: How the Rich Dodge Taxes and How to Make Them Pay

Written by the economists Gabriel Zucman and Emmanuel Saez, "The Triumph of Injustice" is filled with lucid charts showing how, over the past 50 or so years, inequality has radically increased....

Zucman's solution is similar to his fix for multinational tax dodging: a global minimum tax. The idea is straightforward. Countries would agree that no matter where a billionaire lives, he should pay some small portion of his net worth—say, 2 percent—in taxes each year.

If the billionaire already paid that much in income tax, he wouldn't owe anything more. But if he has moved to a country with a lower tax rate or found a hole in his nation's tax code, then the billionaire's home country could charge him the difference between the taxes he paid and the minimum rate.[1]

There are details in the proposal for the world's finance ministers to iron out, of course. And we won't erase inequality just by asking billionaires to give a bit more money back to the countries that fund their employees' education and health care. But, as Zucman writes, "it is a necessary first step."

Zucman deserves a front-row seat in whimsy about money. His idea about how to make the rich pay more taxes is so whimsical it deserves a prize. If I can't be counted on not to take a bargain on the streets of Mexico at a garage sale, who would imagine tax reform? Plus, we have been carefully taught to hate taxes, to hide money from the government, and to trick it into thinking we are paying all we "can." If middle class people are sly with the government, won't rich people be much smarter? They have so much more to gain in scamming the tax system.

You can't dance without a first step. You can't even wiggle without a first move. In a crisis as large as the one we face in our hearts and behaviors about inequality, something that doesn't really hurt billionaires is a great idea. It's not even that whimsical. It is the height and depth of realism. It might even help the 94 percent get excited about ways to stop condemning the 6 percent. It is fully bipartisan in that sense. If it is "all about the money," let's get a hold of the money.

Vacations, Anyone?

You might have heard of Arthur Frommer's guidebook *Europe on 5 Dollars a Day*. As Frommer reflected on his lifework, he remembered well. Each was a learning from travel. What was the point of traveling? Not leisure but learning. Not bargains but knowledge of the self in relationship to the other. It almost sounds like community.

Frommer was a lawyer, and a good one. He was also in the US Army in Europe, where he learned you could book a flight on a cargo jet pretty much every evening if you wanted to. He would show up at the airport, and if the plane was going to Scandinavia, he'd hop on. He got his first bargain courtesy of the US Air Force military transit system. Unlike my bargain, it was fair and generative.

He got another lesson by being hard on places that were ugly, like Branson, Missouri. He not only omitted such places from his guidebooks; if they were ugly, he would shout them out.

He knew how to be hard on a place, like Jesus knew how to call a viper a viper. Or Jimmy Buffet knew how to insult a saltshaker.

Frommer also took one whole city off his list because it wouldn't allow a gay-oriented cruise ship to dock there.

Also, he wanted nothing but to learn from the experience of travel. To him, it wasn't for leisure. It was higher education. He wanted to be turned upside down, just like we were at a garage sale.

I never thought I was ever going to be a travel writer. I was just having a wonderful time traveling on meager funds, but having an experience, it was turning me *upside down,* this direct contact with the life of Europe, with people, seeing all sorts of strange ideologies and lifestyles and approaches and politics in 16 different countries, just going every weekend, flying somewhere or taking a train somewhere.

He also couldn't stand first class. He tells the would-be travel writer: write about your hometown first. If you want to have peace of mind about money, you might begin by figuring out how to enjoy your workday as much as you enjoy your vacation. Flip the switch. Make every day delightful and take a couple of weeks off in a bigger way. Vacations are for changing the weather in our heads. They can best be had at home. If we vacate regularly at home, or stay-cate regularly at home, we are very likely to have the rest last longer than Tuesday of the week we are back.

What Is the Difference between Sabbath Keeping and a Vacation?

Sabbath keeping is one-seventh of your time each week, if you observe a traditional Sabbath. On the seventh day, even God rested. Vacations are two to four weeks (or so) and often represent a heavy outlay of cash, one that is saved up over time. Sabbath keeping doesn't cost anything; in fact, often keeping a good Sabbath keeps us out of stores or offline.

A lot of people go to "nature" for vacations. Hiking, fishing, sunbathing. These are things that our forebears did every day for "work." It's almost like we want to be indigenous for a week or two.

Most people stay home for Sabbath or go to church or temple or mosque as part of Sabbath. The absence of expense is the point. There is something free about Sabbath. I often call it a low-cost form of personal entertainment.

Abraham Joshua Heschel wrote the best book about Sabbath. It is called *The Sabbath,* and he defines Sabbath as the "queen of time." He lived as an Ashkenazi Jew in places with new names in eastern Europe. Artisanal communities of his time—right before the Industrial Revolution—had a small-town feel. People worked with their hands. You didn't need to take a digital Sabbath. Or get your car maintenance done. Or find your cell phone. At night, the men read and discussed Torah—just like we do sometimes at a good dinner party. The women met together as well. Very few of them read. On Saturday there was a feast. People made love. They danced, too, just like at a good wedding. A little more money was spent for the Sabbath feast.

Many of us want to turn back the clock on history and move in with these people. What fun it would be. How low our blood pressure would be.

Many people are taking digital Sabbaths, and I've never heard anyone who does say they regretted it. Mostly, they brag and exult. "Less *is* more," they say.

Sabbath keeping exists to empty us. It calms us down. Originally, it was about resting into God's time. If that is a stretch for you, use a secular orientation. It can be whatever you want it to be, even an hour a day for "what you will." The Haymarket "riot" in Chicago changed the world of work. Its slogan was: "8 hours for sleep, 8 hours for work, 8 hours for what you will." Yes, people in 1859 in Chicago commuted to work, but not in cars or subways.

Sabbath is one day a week for what you will; it may be God, it may be an ultimate, or it may be leisure alone. It is *not* work. It is anything that tells work to go away and allows play to enter in. Work is doing what you have to do and play is doing either nothing or what you don't have to do. There is no paycheck attached to Sabbath, only peace of mind.

We aren't going to turn back the blue laws. Nor are we going to close shopping malls on Sunday or Saturday or Friday. Instead, we discipline ourselves not to open their doors. We don't have to slam the door on our way out or by. A quiet refusal to shop or work or "spend" time with someone you don't like being with—any of these—can be enough to provide the spiritual relaxation that Sabbath freely offers.

Rabbi Judith Shulevitz has written beautifully about how we cannot do this by ourselves. Just can't. I agree. The culture must help us. Or a friend or family group must help us. Why do we let our teenagers work on Sundays? Do we have to? No, we do not. "The good that I would do, I do not, and the evil that I would not do, I do."[2] You can't repeat Saint Paul enough.

Is it sinful not to keep some kind of Sabbath regularly? Yes, it is, if we define sin as missing the mark of our true humanity, becoming curved in on ourselves, and self-obsessed to the point of fear and unproductive individualism. It is also very harmful to us and to the earth and to our children, our parents, and each other.

You may have noticed something in these arguments: meditation by meditation. What is good for us is often just good for us. We refrain from doing what is not good for us. What is less expensive is often extremely good for us. The art of money has to do with the art of refusal. We learn to say no, thank you. Jane Fonda is said to have wisely asserted that *no* is a word in our dictionary. Refusal dethrones the arts of acquisition. It makes room for the queen of time. Sabbath trains us over time to enjoy open and empty and clear as much as we enjoy rush and clutter and stuffed closets. Hmm. Do we really enjoy rushing and stuffing and cluttering? Wouldn't it be interesting to find out? Did you ever hear yourself say, "I just need some time off"? Yes, you do.

Even Serious Jobs Need Comic Relief

Enjoying what the day brings as opposed to planning the day is a way of playing at work. Playing at work takes the sting out of work and puts that famous want in what we have. We leave behind the wanting to have something more or different and learn to want what we have. We become more curious each minute about what the day offers as it proceeds. Sometimes we don't even have to prepare for the ridiculous. We just wait for it to show up on its own time.

One Christmas Eve a farmer in Riverhead, New York, on the East End of Long Island dumped a truckload of turnips on the front yard of the First Congregational Church. The turnips fell along the front doorsteps, blocking the sidewalk to the main entrance, making the beautiful wreath look small. It was 4 p.m. and getting dark. The first service was at 5 p.m. We usually had a packed house. A call to the leadership resulted in about six people rushing over, piling all the turnips into the church basement through the windows that hadn't been opened for a long time.

The farmer helped us. He kept saying, "I want to help the poor." He was inebriated.

Some of the turnips started to smell around January 5. Something had to be done with the vegetables, which were now starting to rot.

Most poor people don't like turnips, even though on Thanksgiving the local restaurant sells out their version of mashed turnips.

The church council held a special session about the turnips. We had a good contact at News 12 Long Island and decided to use it. That's how the Turnip Recipe and Bake-off Contest started. We had a soup kitchen in our church at that time, and the people who ate with us on Wednesday nights helped out. We made turnip sauce, turnip cake, turnip tart, turnip torte, turnip souffle, turnip soup. The winning recipe, first place, went to Dr. Warren Goldstein, my husband, whose turnip fries are now a family staple.

We were flooded with turnips, just like some of us are flooded with asks in our in-box. Being flooded is a common experience. There is just too much of everything. We can't even see the front door, so blocked is it by the excess of others, which joins our own excess. We may not be able to stop the excess. It may be a permanent part of our twenty-first-century experience. If so, the job becomes to make lemonade out of lemons, humor out of the misguided gifts people dump on us, turning turnips into turnip fries.

I learned a lot about the turnip farmer's work and his way of relaxing. He joined us at the contest and had a pretty good recipe of his own.

One Thanksgiving eve at another former church of mine, the First Congregational Church in Amherst, I was packing up my office, again at dusk. Again, I learned a lot about work from another kind of worker. Another inebriated man showed up with an odd gift. He was a local doctor. He plopped a not very well-packaged turkey down on my desk, and some of the blood got onto my paperwork. Again, the cause of this absurd generosity and not-so-well-received gift came out of a good intention. Of course, he wanted to help the poor. Who doesn't?

I told him to walk, not drive home. I thought about putting the turkey into the refrigerator, only to think maybe I knew a family who might still need one. Although, truthfully, even most poor people get a turkey by Thanksgiving eve. I called the family I knew, and the lady of the house said sure. I thought I could drive up the hill to the town where she lived, only to go outside and realize it had started to snow. I called a local cab driver, who said sure, for twenty bucks he'd take the bird up the hill. I gave him the money and off the turkey went up the hill, sitting on the back seat. I put it in a better plastic bag so it wouldn't drip. About an hour later I was safely home thinking about side dishes and turkeys and weird forms of last-minute generosity when my phone rang. It was the lady from the hill town. She said, "Where are the sides?"

Generosity runs amuck. Not just because these two good men were drunk. They were just confused about generosity.

Generosity is something you do for yourself to help yourself get aligned with the golden rule. Generosity is something you do because you live by gift and not by get yourself. People who live to get, like my lady who also wanted side dishes, can't be generous. They can only commit evil and nuisance and expense. Not all generosity is good. Some of it is just nuts. Like the turnips. Or the turkey. Or the sides.

What is the antidote to flooding, like being overrun with just about everything? Or, as T. S. Eliot put it so well, being "distracted from distraction by distraction"?[3] There is too much "ness" afoot. Too much asking. Not even Noah or rainbow or hope that we will ever do anything but drown in rotting turnips or mistaken, misplaced guilt that reduces giving. We can even be generous as a form of "getting."

We can run into generosity run amuck while working or playing or just being. You never know what is going to happen when you get out of bed in the morning.

So, if you are flooded in any way, by too many demands or too little peace, or the failure of your panic abatement plan, relax. (Don't you hate people who tell you just to relax?)

I love the writer Tony Cohan, who wrote *On Mexican Time*: "Each week we work on the house a little less and live in it a little more."[4] When the word becomes fresh among us, we aren't desperate to give and we don't litter the church with turnips or the pastor's desk with bloody birds. We turn our fear into hope, our anxiety into peace, our distractions into focus. We give at our work out of a fullness that does not fear. We receive our play out of fullness that does not fear. We enjoy the sides but don't demand them. We are happy with what we have when we have it.

I will conclude with a line from the menu of Trinciti Red Bar in Brooklyn, a Trinidadian restaurant: "Each noodle generously glossed by cheese, butter and cracked pepper. Pumpkin Curry potatoes also."[5] These are great sides. Very few of us will ever have them. But we know they are there.

6

The Spell of Money and What We Have Lost

How did it come about that money could become so much more important than relationships, community, or religion? How did Mammon win over good—and God? What made us give up the Sabbath and allow our children to work on Sundays or play soccer instead of eating a really good meal or singing with each other? What made us give up the hard-won "8 hours for work, 8 hours for sleep, and 8 hours for what we will," the victory chant of the 1859 Haymarket riot in Chicago? What made us let go of the day's pattern and our need for sleep? What was so good about money and more of it that we left extended families behind and went out to live a nuclear way in tracks and tracks of suburban boxes? What happened to the weekend? Where did it go?

Yes, Maggie Smith famously said in her role on *Downton Abbey*: "What is a weekend?" She was rich and idle. That's why she got to say it.

Why did so many of us start substitution of money for time or money for family or money for fun or money for sleep? Did we ever really say goodbye to our great-grandparents? Why did we abandon the native lands on behalf of a new so-called native land? Were we really that poor there? Apparently, the answer is yes.

Those of us with European descent went from a God-saturated culture to a *Deus Absconditus* situation. Hidden God. Many of us still believe in God but have no architectural, psychological, educational, familial, or ritual behavior to account for our well-hidden, faintly beating "spirituality." How do I know this? Because most of my days are spent talking with real people who don't know which kind of God they don't believe in—and therefore don't know which they might choose if they even saw any pictures of that "kind" of God somewhere in some room they'd like to be in. God 3; Mammon 11 is the score.

Spiritual injury abounds. Religious institutions are as much a joke as Congress or health insurance or public gatherings. They/we don't do what they/we say they/we are doing. Hypocritical is our middle name.

Before you throw the sarcastic nostalgia knife at me, hear me out. I know I am using broad strokes; most people think in equally broad strokes. We need summaries of our anxieties to understand them.

We made most of these changes because of an international population explosion that reduced the capacity of our "native" land to feed us. We also made these changes because of some fervent hope that things marital or familial might be better if we just moved. And yes, nostalgia is longing for a place that never was.

Cain killed Abel. Families were not ever places of peace and quiet. Ask Tevye from *Fiddler on the Roof*: "Do I love her?" We are not the only generations to face into change and loss. Nonetheless, we are facing into rapid changes and major losses. Ancient peoples created apotropaic symbols. Apotropaic means "to ward off evil spirits." They were also afraid, like we are afraid. They used real masks; we just wear masks over our faces, saying what we think we are supposed to say and not saying things we're not supposed to say.

Women got a little bit of a fairer shake in these migrations, but nothing fully changed for us. We still do one-third more domestic or caring labor than the other kind of people. Plus, our day job. I wear that caring labor as a badge of honor, but I also get tired, tired, spiritually tired.

Still, and nevertheless, we made a lot of moves, most of us, and never properly grieved them. Proper grief has phases. We are angry we had to move. We are lost in our new place. We don't know the language. We grieve the loss of patterns. We are mistreated by those who got there before us.

Current immigrants show us these things—but most people also know them in their heart. There is almost no one now who didn't come from somewhere else long ago. What we know in our heart is a kind of loss that is masked by the replacement theory of a better life, with more *things* surrounding us than *relationships*. Things tried to replace relationships, and they have failed. Mammon replaced God and God got lost somewhere. By God, I mean, at least, that which is larger than me or mine. The transcendent of the flatness. The alpha and the omega. These are also broad strokes, and they are mightily needed to make meaning out of the much-coveted melody between body and Spirit.

For those who were forced to come here on slave ships, these losses are even more deeply buried. You need a digger, the kind they used to put a foundation up on a new building in Manhattan, to get to the bottom of a place to start building. You also need a leg up or a ladder, and most of the people around you are pushing you down, every time you get a leg up or dig in firm.

That fervent hope that we could have a better life pushed us out of meager, scarcity-filled lives. Most of us didn't even know we were poor since everyone else seemed about the same. The very rich—who now populate the billboards, the government, and our hearts—were too far away to matter. They also weren't 4 to 6 percent of the world's population and growing in proportion. Some of us really do want to become like them. Or, more precisely, we sure don't want to be like us.

The dream of a better life has disappointed us. Many more now in the United States have a "better life," and watch school shootings on our wide-screen TVs as cars run into New Year's Eve celebrations, while working around the clock to pay off the TV and the car. We watch our neighbors' houses burn down in California fires and say things like "God must be pissed." We are also pissed, ourselves.

What Happened to Our Weather?

Forest fires. Smoke and haze. Plastic molecules found in our babies' bodies. Increased rates of cancer. Decreased rates of fertility. Weather used to be a dull topic. Now, you wonder where you can live and not get flooded or burned or experience some other plague or apocalyptic, unexpected happening. Like a sinkhole in Florida. Or trees falling on the Canadian border. "World's hottest day was today." And then tomorrow. There is nothing dull about the weather today.

I have a confession. I am a fundamentalist about the environment. I see the evidence everywhere, every day that we are devolving as a species. The bill at the end of every meal is way too big. We no longer engage in species survival. We engage in species devolution. We put our money toward the latter and cheap out on the former. Yes, I pick up litter everywhere I go. I recycle what I can. I hate plastic bottles with a sinful vigor.

I'm a complete relativist about most everything. Regarding plastic water bottles, I am rigid. I love water fountains. They are so communal an invention. I love what airports are doing to keep water bottles fillable after so-called security requires us to waste water. I love how easy that change was. It constitutes a narrative change as well as a material change. Both the fountain and the airport show us how easy it is to do the right thing. They suggest a little bit of effort and infrastructure on behalf of a lot of saved water bottles. Yes, people still buy water bottles in airports. We seem to think water bottles are an accessory, like a scarf. We like the individualized hold rather than the group drink. We love the individuality and convenience of the plastic water bottle because it conforms to our main values, of individualism and convenience. We don't see how much these values are embedded in our understandings of money and how much it matters. We pay a lot for the dominance of money. It is quite inconvenient and threatens our very personhood, regularly. Individuals, like societies, need to breathe, to drink, to see. We are devolving by destroying our own air and food and sight.

Imagine copying the airport shift around packaging as well.

The packaging on the food I buy adds an average of 13 percent to the price of the food in the package. Usually, the packaging is like my worst enemy, the water bottle. It is plastic. Sometimes you can't even open the package because it is so tightly wound. You need a knife and fork to get to your food before you can even eat it.

It takes a few minutes to understand how individualized these so-called conveniences are. Why can't we bring our own buckets to buy our beans or rice or olives or whatever we need? Why is food so personal that it doesn't even really taste that good most of the time?

A final note on how costly the damage is that we have done to our weather. And I don't just mean middle class houses on California hills, although their plight certainly moves me and many.

I have some sadness for my grandchildren, who will surely not breathe air as delicious as mine has been or drink water as pure. They will be lucky to live half as well—assuming that my way of life is good in the first place, which it may not be at all, if you do any whole-cost accounting, like Canadian Hazel Henderson does. How much does the packaging and the plastic really cost? Is it as cheap as the price glued to the package says it is?[1]

My sadness for my grandchildren is minor compared to my sadness about the earth. I know that the individualism that has put money on a throne is very expensive. To the earth. To the children of the earth, and not just mine. The rents are just too damn high. And we think they are necessary. They are not. They are excessive. We are stealing nature from our grandchildren.

God's grace allows me to live. I am also very sad, as you can see. Maybe you are too? My enforced lifestyle offends me, my offspring, the earth I love, and God's grace. Does anybody see a reason to continue living the way we do? Is there any way out? That is my question. It is not just about dethroning money or Mammon, which I would love to do. It is about the suicide that joins the murder that joins the devolution.

And I haven't even mentioned cars yet.

The way we use energies of all kinds is harmful to ourselves, our children, our grandchildren, our ancestors' hopes for us, and the earth. It is a devolution that we have chosen because we think we have no other choices. We have plenty of choices. We just must pull the plugs on the choices others have made for us. We are trapped in packaging for now. And water bottles for now. And cars for now. But we don't need to stay there. Money is a form of energy, not a cage or a prison. We don't have to let it slowly drip into our weather and our life. We can turn off some faucets to turn others on. We can turn off an excess of lights to get to a place of sufficient life.

Assess Less Ness

Jesus warned against greed and covetousness, or the desire for more. He said, "Beware of all covetousness. For a man's life does not consist of the things he has" (Luke 12:15).

In *American Bulk: Essays on Excess,* by Emily Mester, we hear: "The constant assessment of daily life is among the all too familiar but strange developments." Rate the doctor. Rate the trip. Evaluate the preacher. Five-star hotel. Three-star hotel....

Mester asks us to answer: Are we finding meaning in all the merch? How many more storage units do we need? And what would happen to us spiritually if life had another set of rewards? Yes, many go shopping and call it retail therapy. Others gladly tell you that they are guilty because they are taking the day off at a spa. What would the right relationship to things look like?

Might it be indigenous in behavior? The word—from the Latin *indigena*, meaning "native," "sprung from the land"—has been used in English since at least 1588, when a diplomat referred to peoples in Siberia as "Indigenæ, or people bred upon that very soil." Did indigenous people assess everything? Or was there something else going on? Are we today not also native to our place and sprung from its land? How much did we colonize our way out of an identity? Can you repair an identity by changing your behavior?

There is so much good about us 19th or 119th generation of migrants, still migrating. I am not talking about people standing at the border today, but all of us who move around. We would never be able to feed all of us without industrial agriculture. Or educate all of us without computers. Soon we will add to our capacity the AI ability to punch-in all the variables and see much better answers for cancer, climate, and much more.

Likewise, there is pretty good biblical evidence that people were violent to each other right after the so-called first peoples of Adam and Eve. Or that people coveted material goods. See the passage above. Tribal warfare dominates the First Testament. Indigenous people were not without conflict. They too mistrusted spiritual experiences and knew enough to be afraid as well as happy about them.

They did live closer to nature. They did not think of nature as something to overcome or evaluate or assess or buy and sell. It was closer to them. Many of us settlers and colonizers seem to regard food as something that comes out of a can or a plastic container. Grocery *prices* are driving people crazy. There might be more there than the price, like the quality or the land from which topsoil was stolen.

We can *still* be closer to nature if we learn to eat our spinach with more gladness.

I, like many, subscribe to *Smithsonian* magazine. It's almost a rite of passage to take our children to the Smithsonian museums. In the January/February *Smithsonian* of 2025, I was astonished to see the indigenous values being renovated for use today. The first story was "Listening to the Land," about an inventive composer who is on a mission to evoke Virginia's past through a strange medley of sounds. He was putting together the night sounds of insects and the way the wind blows through the trees. I'm betting many of us would like to listen in. The second story, "The Ness of Brodigan," is about "what the stones know." Written by Peter Ross, the story is about the Orkney Islands and how much we are like and not alike Neolithic peoples. The story ends with a quote from Nick Card, who lives there. Author Ross is trying to congratulate him for what he has done, as a watcher and guardian of the Ness. He knows that Card might not like such a whimsical description of himself. Card responds, "You don't own the land. You don't own the house. You are just here for a fleeting moment in the history of this landscape. So, a guardian? Yeah, I'd go with that."

This self-assessment by Card measures himself against people of all time. It is a highly repeatable way of thinking, even today. We don't need to own the land privately or even the house. Most of our houses have had more than one owner over time. We don't need to assess yesterday's meeting or meal or service appointment for our cars. What we need to do is be guardians of our time and space. We can be as indigenous as our forebears any time we want to think large and grand about what it means to be a small human. We have river keepers and sound keepers and lighthouse keepers and more. We can learn to keep and get the word *indigenae* back.

Imagine having an ungraded experience. Do the "mountain pose" and push your feet hard and firmly into the ground. It is still there. Do tai chi and raise your arms to the sky and acknowledge the wind. It blows. Drink water from a glass and never touch another plastic bottle. Don't do it because it will fix the environment. Light one candle, not a forest of Christmas lights. The environment is not for fixing. Stephen Gould wisely argued, "Nature is not for the human. Nature is for nature." Do it out of regard for the drops and the sprinkles and the taste and the glory of water.

Break the bonds of assessment and get an A plus in life instead of flunking it.

Gravity and Capitalism

Gravity is a fact and capitalism is a fiction. Gravity is also a beautiful fiction, enjoying a multiplicity of levels, the transcendent and the grounded, factness and alluring allusions. Grave. You can't get out of the grave. Eventually you go down. Grave. Like many truths. A person of gravity. Someone you must consider because you know you have to consider them. They have gravity. They keep things. They guard things. They don't own things. They create ownerships, communal owning of things in common. They especially create ideas and stories that we don't and can't own. We can borrow and "rent."

Capitalism acts like a fact. It has lots of reasons to boast. Capitalism does improve the human condition, materially. It does respond to one of the most interesting parts of being human: our drive to get better, to improve, to make hay while the sun shines. It creates excitement and buzz. The New York Stock Exchange comes to mind. It funds our most interesting medical and scientific discoveries. It shows us what we can do. It gets us out of bed in the morning and moves us to new thoughts, new movies, new books, new dances, new curiosities.

Capitalism always should have a small c. There are many kinds of capitalism, some more or less usurious, some more or less conceited, some more or less understood. B Corps come to mind. Worker-owned companies like Costco come to mind. Small-c capitalism breeds variety in every generation, especially those that don't hoard but spread, like a Carnegie, or a Rockefeller, or a Ford. These big-name foundations do good, intentionally, as though that were an inherent part of capitalism's job description. Even Walmart has a foundation.

The fact is that capitalism has a decent track record—even though people on all sides of American politics still say "it's all about the money" at the end of way too many conversations. Even people who praise capitalism offer that as the catch-all explanation for that which goes wrong. Like its assault on the earth, wind, and rain, through fracking, enforced automobile driving, polluting the water, and so much more. Like plastic. Like meaning on the job. Like intergenerational squabbles. Like lost humor and joy. People don't like capitalism but really don't like people who criticize it, either. The presumed consent people give to capitalism is a charade. They just don't know where the exit is in its on-fire theater.

For me, capitalism's problem is Shakespearian or related to gravity's innocent mottos that "pride comes before a fall" and "what goes up must come down." Capitalism has become too big for its britches. It doesn't know how to land the fall.

One of the main spiritual jobs of the human is to land the fall. We are all Olympians, when it comes to our own very speck-like lives. Our self-consciousness makes us all large. Landing the fall means at least not relying too much on our own press releases. It means avoiding pride on behalf of joining and building family and community. It means what Martin Luther meant as sin, *Incurvatus in se*, curving in on yourself. We are to curve out, not in. Toward God and each other. Pride is the barrier to our landing the fall. We think we are better than gravity. We are not. We will die. We will fall in the ground or into the stardust. And we will make mistakes. As Mr. Card says, we are only here on this largeness for a very small period of time.

Capitalism today does more harm than good and doesn't know it. That pride is killing it and us.

I saw a compelling story in a movie, *Félicie*. A ballerina wants to learn how to leap and is told the only way to do so is to land the fall. A former dancer adopts her. She is to practice by jumping into a puddle—not around it, but into it—in a way so the water doesn't splash. The former dancer teaches her how to clear and open the space. I wonder if this is how we land the inevitable fall of money, while appreciating what it has given us. We don't splash. Perhaps we conserve the puddle so the next generation has a clear and open space? We dance beautifully into its opening and clarity. We don't destroy the puddle on our way down.

I can imagine thinking of office conflicts and family spats as puddles, begging us to jump into them and be glad about the turbulence—just long enough to land the fall and not disturb the water as we negotiate, talk, calm, imagine together.

Gravity is a scientific fact. Capitalism is a human construct that tries to be absolute and ultimate, and it is neither. It is just a puffed-up construct. Its money is just a form of energy. A beautiful form of energy, but just that. It has no right to universal truth or whatever else it purports to be. It is here not to harm the puddle but to keep it safe for the next clarity and opening.

Capitalism Enforces and Forces Itself on Us

The biggest complaint I have with small-c capitalism is that it takes up all the space. It forces itself upon us. It seduces us by advertising into believing its tale is the only tale. There are many more stories possible.

In the introduction, I offered a small shift by showing how one community used the benefits of usury to redistribute wealth. Here is a less inspiring, if equally interesting, example.

The Community Cab Company (CCC) started in New Haven, Connecticut, after a Yale student was murdered on the way from campus to the train station. It used a million-dollar individual contribution matched by two downtown churches that put in $1 million each of their endowment. Yes, many churches spend their endowment before the rainy day, not after it. Usury yields interest, which can be used for good or ill. That initial $3 million bought twelve brand-new cabs.

Why was there no cab company in New Haven? Why did students and citizens have to walk so far to the train station? Or get a private car that charged enormously to get a kid to the babysitter, or a grandmother to her doctor's appointment? The reason was very simple. The owner of the cab company used the decline of his rolling stock over two decades to decrease his personal taxes, and then he walked away. His behavior was not exactly usurious, although if he hadn't had the money from his investment, he wouldn't have been able to pay the lawyers who helped him game the tax system to use private wealth increase to hurt his neighbors. Private property joined personal interest, supported by government chaos, to cause a murder and daily stress for many people. The owner of the cab company who put personal gain/good over public gain/good hurt a lot of people on his way to wealth. He had choices he didn't use. Maybe he was personally happy. At what cost? Extractive capitalism hurts our neighbors; replenishing capitalism helps them, as well as us as individuals.

CCC was designed to make money (usurious) for the private investor and the two churches. It guaranteed 5 percent per year. The company was worker owned, and it intended to pay back the initial investment over time. It was put out of business after the first year, sold to a private owner, and now there are plenty of cabs (plus Uber and Lyft) in New Haven. Why was it put out of business? We do-gooders missed one important matter. Taxis are a regulated industry, like water and electricity. If we could run a business that charged less to pay more, both in returns and in wages, which we were trying to do, then would that also make other taxi companies that were privately owned have to do the same? We hoped so. Anyway, in a widely publicized case (for which we have no photos, because this was before photos were allowed in court in the 1980s) we lost. The utilities and taxicab industry had a lot of well-dressed suits who knew regulation. We had one lawyer, an expert in housing. We also had on our side of the aisle several hundred so-called welfare queens, elderly people in wheelchairs and children who didn't have cars, plus our twelve original employees and a lot of church folk who loved the idea that their endowment was alive instead of stagnant.

The scene was downright biblical. The court decided: "You cannot *not* make a profit on taxi business in Connecticut." If we were able to make interest on our money but not a profit on our money over that interest, then the regulated water and utility businesses might have to do the same thing. Imagine not being able to make a profit selling people water and electricity. That would be a crime in the usurious world. Notably, the entire original investment was returned, without interest, to the two churches and the individual donor.

Being good with money is both doing good with money and letting money do good. There were other options here than a stark divide in the community between good and bad and mutual recrimination. "We" do-gooders and "they" bad-doers were in a fictional fight for the white hat. Watch out for any sentence that says "we" and "they"; there is a lot of "they" in "we," and vice versa. There are plenty of places in between, where we can do more good and less bad over time. The Community Cab Company was a good start. It was a picture of what is possible, even if it only lives as a testimony to how to get smarter, longer.

CCC was a witness to what is possible. Some things work and others don't. Purpose persists and remains pursued in failure and success. Alliteration means there is power in trying and power in succeeding. How often a day should we encourage someone to "keep on keeping on"? Seven times seven? I think so. The day we lose the ability to imagine a less usurious future is the day we consent to the sin and forswear a primary relationship with the divine.

This steadiness is great work. If the *wages* of sin are death, the *wages* of primary relationship with created promise are golden.

7

Breaking the Spell: Catching Ourselves Doing Something Right

Breaking the spell means understanding that it is a spell.

What we have done right is to learn from our mistakes. What we have done right is to think and to see and to pause and collect what we know from our experience and the experience of those whom we know and even love.

When we reflect or pray or pause for a minute or two, we say to ourselves, I don't have to live this way. I can live a little bit different. Differently? We become imperfectionists, which is also a subtle challenge to the rules of the systems. We do our best. We let our best be good enough. We understand that we will still likely drive, eat out of packages, drink out of water bottles as infrequently as possible. We will signal to ourselves and each other that we don't belong to the systems, but they belong to us. We made them and we can change them. Breaking the spell means understanding that it is a spell.

Our understandings need be spoken out loud to friends and families. We can explain ourselves to each other so that we don't turn prayer and action-reflection into forms of willpower. That is another version of internalized capitalism. "If I just worked harder, I'd have a better job. Why? It's all up to me." It's all up to us. Not me or you but you and me together.

What is a spell? It is a habit of mind. It is a habit of behavior. It is the ether. It is in the water. It is where we live and breathe. It is like that overused word *addiction* or the other overused word *trauma*. We'd like to think that we are our own persons, but mostly we are not. We are what each other believe to be true. Understanding that money is a kind of spell can help us rebuild the communities that might be a little bit happier than those we currently create. Yes, we create them every day. Every time we say "it's all about the money," we recreate a community that hurts. Every time we say "it's all about us," we recreate a community that helps.

> We can renew and repair the environments we are trying to destroy.
> We can assess less and appreciate more.
> We can live closer to the land and not romanticize it but enjoy having our feet on the ground.
> We can create taxicab companies and write books that people will ban.
> We can take risks that involve losing money because we don't want that much more than we have.

◆

I spent most of my last holiday with a five-year-old, one of those short people who knows just about everything. She gave me a short course on epistemology. Surely, science- and fact-based thinking have given us a lot! Also, they are used to defend the kind of capitalism that hurts us. They could also be used to defend that capitalism by opening space for other forms of thinking. Faith and fact are not opposites; they are friends.

We watched *Into the Woods*, a musical by Stephen Sondheim. She knew all the songs by heart. At one point, I asked her how this was ever going to end. "*Bubbe*, you can't know the end till the end. Don't you know anything about fiction?" I countered, "I am an English major. I know a lot about fiction. I even know the difference between fiction and fact." She continued, "Don't tell me you don't believe in angels? Or witches? Or spellllllllllls?"

If only she knew how well trained I was to *not believe* in the extraterrestrial and to overdepend on the terrestrial. I am as enchanted by the facts of the earth and the fictions of the earth. I am enchanted by the connection between stardust and the human genome, the size of the cosmos, the fact that there *is* electricity in the first place. I am a friend of Einstein's, especially because he said, "There are two kinds of people, those who don't believe in miracles and those who know everything is a miracle."

What is great about our moment in time is how much miracle making science is doing. The cell phone. AI. Evolution and devolution.

What are also great are the stories movies are telling our children and grands. Anza is right. You can't know the end till the end. Fact meet fiction! We don't know how the human story is going to end. We do know that we enjoy both fact and fiction. We love to tell each other stories. We love to let fact have a conversation with fiction and to have fiction win in the end.

Creating a story that it is all about us and not all about the money is restoring and restorying. It is what the people in the woods were doing.

You can't know the end till the end. You can predict that before the end comes things will get very hard. The musical needs the trouble to move ahead. All sorts of challenges appear to our heroes and heroines. Conflict is impact. It's actually very good. It's how we grow. The importance of the word *emergency* is to emerge, to learn from it. That's why it's terribly important to pause and go slow and let conflict pull you to good conclusions, ones that reflect the facts and your dreams.

Conflict is good. Trouble is good. They drive the plot. Conflict is the only way we learn. Without conflict, we remain stupid and people leave after the first act of the show. With conflict, like mine in South Dartmouth two days before Christmas, we have repeated AFLEs: "Another F … Learning Experience." That's my name for growth.

The whole town of South Dartmouth overdoes itself every Christmas, lighting up everything, and I do mean everything, even the stop signs. Is this excess joyous or an insult to the environment? You decide. Do I go all the way to thanking the distressed environment for being my teacher? Not often. I might go there more often.

◆

We also watched *Wicked*. G-Linda Glinda, the good witch, had to know that Elfie/Elphaba, the bad witch, had one angelic experience after another. First Glinda, sly and manipulative, donates her boyfriend to Elphaba's sister for a prom date. Elphaba, moved by the rare generosity, gets Glinda a place in the sorcery class. Glinda returns the favor by giving Elfie a makeover. They are so moved by each other that they change their names. One gift leads to another and another, and the next thing they know they are fighting the evil powers of the universe *together*.

The plot turns by gifts. The gospel story plot also turns by gifts—with a little punishment thrown in for not understanding the power of a gift.

It's very hard for those of us who live in this kind of time to understand either fact or fiction, dominated as we are by excessive information, excessive stuff, and excessive possibilities. We are overdone and overcooked. We don't even taste good to ourselves.

Could the head of a major insurance company be assassinated on the day the Christmas tree was lit uptown in Manhattan? Yes. Could the American public be so angry that they denied him the usual *I am so sorry for your loss* and went straight to their own complaints? We didn't even say we were worried about each other. We were worried about our own health, our own possible sicknesses, and how they make us broke. Broke meaning money, not body. Even fear is individualized.

We are sometimes so angry and scared that we deny humanity even to sinners. (The people in South Dartmouth are not any more sinful than I. We all participate in overuses. We don't know how not to.) Likewise, the people who gouge us when we are sick, the health insurers who are fear insurers, are also human. We are all in this *together*. The sinners are also us.

Many of us have given the speech about dehumanization. First, we dehumanize, then we use hate speech; next thing we know we have decided that the head of a major corporation is less than human.

Way opens, says the Quakers. Yes, it does. Right after we have another AFLE.

How are we going to get through one climate catastrophe after another? By wrestling with our better angels. And not knowing the end till the *end*. And learning to say *we* instead of just *me*.

I highly recommend www.socialchangeinitiative.com/narrative-change for both tired scientists and tired English majors.

Please visit us with a spell-breaking spell, oh God, and grant us a right spirit within us. Amen.

◆

We are all migrants now, maybe moving toward each other.

Migration meant loss and it also meant gain. What went right is relief from the small world. What went right is what I have always imagined was the divine purpose in the first place. We are to become all mixed up. Instead of *miscegenation* being a bad word, it is on its way to being a good word, *if and as the dream becomes relational*.

Tribalism is having a field day these days because so much of it is lost. The United States will tip to majority "minority" in a decade or less. Nomads, like me, have new respect. I was already Irish and Dutch and German, even before I got here and married a Lithuanian Jew. I became a Christian pastor who has three grown children, two of whom are Jewish and one of whom is agnostic. Imagine what's going to happen to their children, said my great-grandmother as she rolled over in her Lutheran grave. She was never called *Bubbe*, my name as a grandmother because of becoming an honorary Jew by marriage.

The human is simultaneously evolving and devolving—as the birth rate declines and gender fluidity becomes accepted. Those who still can't stand that freedom will die off soon enough and will be replaced by a rapid kind of social change, one that must have biological as well as social and cultural roots.

What will happen to money as culture blends and people are more fully aware of how many worlds there are? You can count on money and the 6 percent who have it to protect it with all their heart and mind and soul, the words we used to use for catechetical instruction. You can also count on culture simultaneously improving its capacities. Many will turn to fear instead of amazement.

I am profoundly affected by one Ted Talk. It is titled "The Danger of a Single Story," told by Chimamanda Ngozi Adichie. She says that God made multiple stories and did so intentionally. That's why we have the good voodoo and the bad voodoo, alongside Christians with Christ and Christians with Jesus and Jews who like Jesus and Muslims who like Jews. Ah. That would help, wouldn't it?

We need to help religion itself get unlocked, unstuck, unfrozen so we ourselves as ordinary people can become unlocked, unstuck, unfrozen. We are frozen in the ice of individuality. We could melt into community—as long as we didn't have to protect ourselves with more money, the best Gods, and thereby inoculate ourselves against the competition. Yes, there are some very wealthy people who would also like to unfreeze. They are not all evil. But like camels trying to get through the eye of a needle, lots of money can be very blinding. I know. I am rich. I don't want to lose what I have. But I do want to spend it well. I don't want to keep it, either. It sours me. Also, Arthur Frommer wisely advised against first class.

Without a breakthrough, the lines at the airport will always be the same. Haste and hurry will overfill our days. We will be in a self-made flood. We will miss out on life, being afraid to lose what we have. I have finally figured out why I pat my pockets so often. I am afraid to lose what I have. At first it was just another downside of the upside of the privilege of being old. It's more than that. It is fear of losing what we have. People confirmed this to me in the last election. People even richer than I talked about how afraid they were of being taxed out of their current very pleasant lives. They held their noses and voted for someone who would refrain from taxing wealth.

One Christmas at the Harford Airport, early in the morning, before I was awake enough to trust my perceptions, I saw the fast and coach lines reversed. I was astonished. It was almost like the Christmas story had taken life before my very eyes. Nobody was competing for a first-class seat in the manger. Nobody had bought their way in. The coach line was going fast and the elite line was going slow.

We can be right in wrong ways and wrong in right ways and wrong in wrong ways but rarely right in right ways. That is beyond our pay grade as people. Becoming right in right ways is becoming more plural and sharing our corner of the one earth vigorously, intentionally, and regularly. "After you," we say in either line. I know that sounds preposterous. It is what neighborliness, community, and the wonderful world beyond individualism look like. Instead of believing that winning makes us better than other people, we can watch how winning turns us into losers. Those funny Abbott and Costello skits come to mind: "After You," or "Who's on First?"

In another life I have the privilege of teaching chaplaincy to Muslim students. As is usual in teaching, I am the student, they are the teachers. We often teach what we need to learn. Due to the great increase in the number of Muslim immigrants in the United States, hospitals, universities, and prisons are all desperate for Muslim chaplains. These students are well trained in their Koran and have the same problems of many Christians in assuming that their religion is the best. To be a chaplain, however, is to learn how to regard your religion of origin with great pride while not overdoing it. You may get to die with a person who is Christian this afternoon, a Jew that evening, and a Buddhist in the morning. You need to know all the last rites, not just a few of them. And you need to know when *not to use* anything traditional at all.

Muslim students often have a very hard time refusing to evangelize. So do Christians. Anyway, back to the story. In any of these chaplain settings, at least half of your population is going to be *none of the above*. They are going to be what we call postsecular people. Shorthand for them is people who read horoscopes, have a great sense of "spirituality but not religion," believe in a vague kind of God, and are as fed up with secularism as they are with religion. These people are the ones prepared to be rehabilitated and dehabituated first. They are less habitual in thought and practice. They are on the edge. They want above all to be sincere about something as important as faith, and they don't want to lie about their faith just to look good. Religious people avoid these people like the plague, and these people avoid religion like the plague. Why? Because of the way that too many Christians use the word *Christ*, and too many Muslims use *Allah*. Our god or the highway. Emphasizing belief in the triumphal God when the very man Jesus, the "son of man and the son of God," didn't talk to people about them having the right faith. He talked about getting them food and water and clothing and unstuck and out of the jails they/we create for them.

Every five hundred years Christianity has a great reawakening. Phyllis Tickle, religion editor of *Publisher's Weekly* for three decades, argued often that every five hundred years the Church has to have a big rummage sale and get rid of stuff. In honor of Christ the King, I'd like to throw out the idea that Jesus is the only way to the ultimate divine Creator. He is a great way. We get there by paying attention to the least and the lost, the God who came down and joined us in redeeming creation. We get to true Spirit by the golden rule, which says, "After me."

Many of us have a serious fear that the human species is devolving. We wonder about our children and where they will get water or shelter, if they can't go outside because it is too hot. We wonder about their children. And we feel strangely impotent about what we might do to help. We see Artificial Intelligence on the horizon and talk to robots pretty much every day on a screen or a phone line. We wonder if it will hurt or help us evolve as a species. This devolution is troubling to our hearts while we drink our morning coffee. Covid-19 jumped on our trouble and exacerbated it. My antidote to this chronic crisis on multiple levels is to seek out the new revelation of God. I believe the power of God's love for the human (and also the burro and the bird) is so strong that God is trying hard to reveal a new way to us. God is not in trouble, we are. God will be fine. God's new revelation is as global as our computer's screen. It is as local as our neighbor next door. It is profoundly glocal and will not be kept to the provincialization of any one religion. Christianity is just one religion. Likewise, Islam, etc. There is a danger in only one story.

One real benefit of capitalism is that it is international and wants to become more so. It will need to learn a new tribalism, not one that pits rich against poor, tribally, but understands the power and beauty of more than one story about everything, including God and Mammon. Money will have to make sure it is not on the throne but on the ground. That's how we will all stay rich and survive. The very word *rich* might well undergo what the words *Jesus* and *American* and *human* all mean.

A Modern Indigeneity

Indigena means living close to the land, as a native on a native land, for one's whole life. That was a great idea for a long time, and then it changed. The earth may not be able to stand the amount of population we now have—unless relationships improve both to it and to each other. If we learn to feed each other, all will be well. I will call myself a thirteenth-generation native on the many different lands where I have laid my head on a mattress, above the ground. I will be indigenous to my land in my imagination, if not in my grocery shopping.

I will acknowledge the land(s) on which I live and respect them and compost my waste on each one. These actions of respect and relationship will allow the land to expand its capacity to feed us. Food is also not the most important matter. We also want the land to sport us, entertain us, challenge us, connect us. All these things are technically possible and can be affirmed by those who want to live well and ensure that all live well.

Boy scouts try to leave the camp site better than how they found it.

A good land acknowledgment for a thirteenth-generation nomad, no matter where they lay their head, is: "I am not the first person on this land, nor will I be the last. I honor my ancestors and my offspring and hope that their life will be as good as mine is. I live in such a way as to fulfill that hope." (You will see many different land acknowledgments throughout this work. That's because there are lots of different lands and ways to acknowledge them.)

The creator never imagined land for a few. The creator imagined land for many and like a good parent, when she died, she wanted the children to know how to get along. I remember watching both my mother and my husband's mother die. In their hearts was one thing: May the wars between the siblings stop. May they find each other. May they take care of each other. Ah.

Indigena means living off the land and the air and the cell phone's energy patterns. *Indigena* means using a microwave, maybe. It doesn't have to be romanticized, as it was never all that romantic. We did lose some things in the migrations. We did not lose everything.

Restoried imaginations can give us feet on the ground and hopes in the sky. We may have improved more than we even know. And if we haven't improved, at least we can improve our dream. If the dream is more money for us and let the rest be forgotten, that is a dangerous dream. It won't raise good children. It won't honor our ancestors. It is surely destroying the land. If the dream becomes more collective, we will have a shot at the very hope we work so hard to realize.

Becoming less dependent on money and things as our validators comes from a religious perspective, one large enough to be true.

E. B. White, already mentioned as coeditor of *A Subtreasury of American Humor*, author of *Charlotte's Web*, and great humor writer, said it this way: "I wake up in the morning, wondering if I should save or savor the world. This makes it very hard for me to plan my day." My confidence that God is issuing new information and new direction all the time is very helpful to me. It allows me to remove some of the weight of the world from my shoulders. Then you can plan a reasonable day. You can rest in a God that is in charge, and not in an imperial way. God needs us! But we and the imperial God are not in charge. We are all in charge. That's what it means that God became human, to show us the way. God made a parable out of community by coming into community with us.

Taking scripture seriously but not literally allows you to enjoy many stories, not just one. Becoming less triumphant means you too don't have to win the personal Olympics, either; just land the fall. There will be many falls along the way. Part of the One Universal Creator God way behind all the other gods is here. The new revelation will mean respect for all faiths, beyond the minimalist Thanksgiving services of the early interfaith years into a much more mature respect and knowledge of one another.

8

Alternative Economies

The Art of Repair: Can Anybody Fix This Thing?

My friend Glynnis, an architect, wants churches to develop repair shops. Broken lamps and broken clocks for starters, and malfunctioning printers and computers for finishers. She wants us to make real the experience of becoming new. Or getting over being broken. Or discarded. Or just crapping up the place by our very useless presence, the way cords infiltrate our floors and become trip hazards.

She wants people to experience Easter, and she thinks we can do it through objects.

She talked me into repairing my old white wooden stool, the one I use to get to the higher shelves. It had some stains on it from some kind of glue, long left behind by some kind of boot. I had used it ugly. One day, thinking about Glynnis and her intelligent doubts about the truth of Christianity and its Easters, I got out some old can that was hiding deep in its tomb in the back of my least favorite closet. It said on it "removes stains." I applied it and a lot of elbow grease and next thing I knew my distressed stool was white as snow.

I had almost bought a plastic one at the Dollar Store about three times for $6.99. But I couldn't quite bring myself to part with the coins. Why was I not restoring the old one? Why was it headed to a landfill, with more plastic coming into my house?

My repair restored my pride, which is, of course, at least as large a sin as doubt or sloth. My pride turned into a parable. Now every time I use the stool, I congratulate myself and look around for something else to clean or dust or refresh.

Many think that capitalism is a kind of sorcery, just like Glynnis regards Christianity. *Sorcery* is an old-fashioned word, like the word *spell*. Today we more often use the word *addiction*. We are bound to something that hurts us, and we can't escape. I think both are right. We have lost hope in repair and hope only for something new. The right new couch or stool or vacation will turn the trick. Many like capitalism because it is a system of strong incentives. It tricks you into thinking it will make you happy. Then you do produce more, work harder, think harder so you can be happier. Glynnis suspects Christianity of the same sorcery.

I think if we looked harder for hidden tools and used a little more elbow grease when it comes to creating parables, then we would truly be happier. God (Something more important than us) will meet us halfway. (Thank you, Bill McKibben, for that version of hope—the hope of God meeting us halfway, as you said in that great Third Act lecture.) We will at least get to the threshold of the closet into which we are locked. We will peek out.

What is it about birds and cages? Is there really a cage just about everywhere waiting for a bird? Why do birds so often self-inflict? I like to repeat this image because most people start shaking their heads "yes" when it appears.

The cover of this book has a swarm, a community of birds, flying in and out of the cage of the dollar sign. I wonder if that is what we really mean by liberation—the ability to come and go? Evenings in Mexico, we often saw five, six, or seven swarms circle our town. They came about fifteen minutes before sunset; then they disappeared. Then they came back. Added, obviously.

One wag argued that aging is like constantly being punished for a crime you didn't commit. C. S. Lewis called it chronological snobbery. He defined it "as the uncritical acceptance of the intellectual climate of our own age and the assumption that whatever has gone out of date is on that count discredited." Such an approach carries two distinct but related dangers: "One, as Arthur Lindsley of the C. S. Lewis Institute put it, 'we need the help of past ages to see our own times more clearly.' And two, we lose the ability to benefit from truths discerned by our predecessors—the wisdom of the ages."[1] In brief, we seek out the new, shiny thing and diminish and demean the old.

C. S. Lewis disliked usury as well. Usury props up capitalism and its love of the new and disdain for the old. He accused all three of the then major religions of being insufficiently critical of usury. They are "quietly" against it. He wanted alternatives.

Have you ever wondered if our widespread prejudice against the old comes from their not being "useful" in a usurious way? Can't earn. Can't pay their own way. Live off the "tit" of Social Security. All gluey and ugly and stained. How could we repair the "crime" of getting old?

Or imagine a national policy on immigration and a simple border policy: let's "take" twice as many people as we can "keep."

That would restore generosity and help people feel better about themselves. Pride. It might even take the sting out of death and reteach our culture how to respect the ancient, the old, the elder. We have a marvelous tradition of receiving people into the United States. Ask the Statue of Liberty. It too regularly needs a polish. It doesn't need to be thrown out.

During Covid-19, I prayed we might find a national purpose large enough to unite us in a common task. Immigration, a mess of an issue with no right answers, could unite us, if we tried harder to be generous and did it together. In *Schindler's List*, the rich man broke down when he realized he might have saved one more family if he had just sold one more of his cars. Are we breaking down and breaking because we don't have a job to do? Maybe our job is repair?

My dog is a border collie. She is only happy when she has a job. Otherwise, she mopes. Imagine a border collie at a border. Or kids playing volleyball over a Mexican–United States border. Or musicians on both sides of the Rio Grande making music together.

Repair shops for the old? Repair shops for stools? I wonder how much money that would save. Or cost? And what would it do for the way I buy pants to cover my varicose veins when I play tennis? Sometimes I'd just like to show them off as signs of blood still coursing.

But I also live in a closet, standing on its threshold, wondering how so much got so broken and can't be fixed.

Thrift Stores

Thrift stores are marvelous. They are a green and low-cost form of personal entertainment. Thrift stores have an abundance of virtues. One, nothing can be greener. They help the environment; help our species survive. Two, they employ the main constituency of most congregations, which is women of a certain age who are vital, funny, beautiful, and know how to have a good time together "doing good." Three, they support the best not-for-profits in the business, religious congregations.

My recent purchases resulted in a non-moth-eaten cashmere sweater and some adorable baby shoes for my latest grandchild. I noted that one Episcopalian shop had hidden political messages embedded in the cookware and sweatshirts. Sneaky and welcome. I won't declare who they were blessing or cursing. Suffice it to say it was closer to my point of view than my mother's.

My mother should have left my father, as I frequently pontificated. He was too mean to her. She was an orthodox Christian, never told me how she voted, although I think it wasn't my way, and believed in marriage in a traditional way.

Despite my advice, which she eventually took, we really enjoyed each other's company, especially while bargain hunting. Our favorite activity was to take two carts and arrive on senior discount day at the ABC store in Minneapolis, when she would pay for everything and I, not yet discounted, would reimburse her with cash. She lived in the cold with my sister, Cathy, also the best affordable housing practice ever discovered.

We marched through the corridors with earnest purpose. If one of us found something good, we would find the other and show it off. Then we'd return to the hunt.

Ellie was a rabid mystery reader, who read about ten mysteries a week. She never heard Krista Tippett's great line, that she could easily give up on murder but not murder mysteries. She also bought Bearington Bears. When she died, we distributed 250 of them, average price $1.99 minus 30 percent on Tuesdays.

That popular song about amazing grace croons, "I once was lost but now I'm found." It is the theme song of thrifting.

Ellie (Eleanor Clara Waterman Osterhoudt) loved a good find and a good bargain. She knew that grace was not a bargain and could be misplaced. When she sang a hymn, like "I Love to Tell the Story," with her clear alto voice, she wasn't talking about books or bears. She was talking about Jesus, whose story held her through violence, hardship, and neglect.

I go to thrift stores most Tuesdays, just to talk with her, find a bargain, and remember her expensive faith and her mysterious frugality.

Some people think I am there for the sweaters. I'm there to be with her.

The Hawk Trail

One season, I drove Route 2, the former Mohawk Trail, to preach at a small church in Shelburne Falls, Massachusetts, every Sunday morning. I come off 91 North at Greenfield and climb the hill. Every one of my first twelve Sundays in 2023 it poured rain. Then there was a deluge, and part of the road just fell down the hill. That was the summer of this awakening as I write. We may already be on the Climate Cliff, the point of no return. June 7 the air turned foul with wildfire fog. Then the constant rain. Then the hill fell.

Communities all over the United States are looking at their monuments and their road names and their public art. Richmond. New Haven. Montgomery. Baltimore. New York. Hudson. Stone Mountain, Georgia. Even Franklin County in Western Massachusetts.

This look in the place mirror makes most of us nervous, but in different ways. Those who want to conserve fear changes of names; those who want to liberate welcome the changes. Both are right, and both are wrong. Refusing the need to be right, while knowing a piece of you is wrong, could go a long way to make us happy in our old and new places. Places are always both old and new; they are always aging and getting younger. They are perpetually renewing, even when interpretations don't so indicate.

What do monuments have to do with money? They are a parable for change. Once something was called this; now we call it that. What was once a proud middle class is now a threatened middle class, put down by well-advertised wealth. Once hard work was considered a virtue, and one that would get a living wage; now it is put down as insufficient, not enough, and needing a "side gig."

Matters like the so-called Indian statues that climb the hill with you on the Mohawk Trail educate. They are both iconic and accessible, larger than life, and mark our passage up and down. They also teach gravity. Even the natives, supposedly praised by having a name, don't like being named by others. We know where we are when we see them. They comfort and then they confront. Many of us saw them when we were ten on our first trip that way, then again when we were seventy on our potentially last trip up that way. Often, they give a good laugh and someone in the back seat says, "Don't they need a war paint job?" or some equally affectionate if weird remark.

Interestingly, the trail was there long before the last century's art. The hawks of many generations circled above and didn't quarrel or even name their places. They didn't know the meaning of the word *their*. They didn't think of private property as a sacred right. Those words are a human invention. Birds sing their songs for themselves; humans try to impress others with how much they "own" or "know."

Old-timers on Cape Cod, where middle-class people could usually afford a vacation, remember when the security system for their front yards on the beach was to build a fire and invite whoever passed by to join them in a sit-down. New-timers put up signs that say "private property," as if someone could own the sea or the sand. These signs moderate themselves sometimes, arguing, "No dogs or fires allowed," and are signed by the beach association. They have no legal standing on the Cape, but they assert a foolish anthropology, like private property or my tax dollar. But at least, if you think the human itself is that important, it gives permission to the so-called "right" for the human to pass without kindling or walking their (their?) dog.

When we try to live beyond the false binary of good and bad about money, we don't really have to fight with each other. We can, but we don't have to. We can put up a sign in our front yard that says come on in. Or we can put up a sign that says stay out. We can do small things that break the binaries in small ways while testifying in larger ways to questions as large as who owns what and why. We can be YIMBY—yes in my back yard—and find community or NIMBY—not in my back yard—and be lonely. Those are the choices.

People who put up signs and think they own their land or trail or name of their trail or their dog are insecuring themselves, while thinking they are securing themselves. The only possible security is in deep, respectful, trusting community, the kind that invites in rather than shuts out. Knowing your neighbors, even the ones who come in via Airbnb, matters. Yes, some people will drink beers and drop cans and have reckless fires; others will leave rubbers behind or other, less interesting detritus. Can you stop them? No. Can you get to know them? Yes. Over time. Even saying hello can help.

Back to the trail. Naming it the Mohawk Trail was both a kindness to the former so-called owners and a dog marking. Now it is ours.

The way to be both right and wrong, safe and not so, is to get in touch with the great paradox of time. Places last. They change. They last and change. Humans need to learn to think like birds and fly over with delight. The less concrete we pour on things, the better. So how about a *land acknowledgment* that is not good enough for the hawk or its trail? Something that hails the sunrise, that bridges the flowers, that greens the fields, that deers the fields, that sunders the land, that does less naming and more enjoying? What about now renaming the Mohawk Trail something new that will only last a century or so? What about hawking the trail?

Or putting in your email signature: *I acknowledge the land where I stand now, which some call the Mohawk Trail, others call the Hawk or the Trail, and still others call home. I acknowledge that people before me called this place home and those after me will name it home too. I share this home with the hawks and the people who came before and who come after.* That acknowledgment makes sure not to act like you own anything, and that is the important, securing part. It's neither right nor wrong. Add self-righteousness to the way you say your land acknowledgment, and you will ruin it. What we call capitalism ruined itself by excessive enforcement of its way as the *only way*.

At our little church, Trinity, in Shelburne Falls, people said, "We have a bench in our garden." What a great security system. What a great name. How proud we are to invite others to come and kindle. There, we remember our past and look forward to our future, as the hawks sail regardless of the name we use to name. Does our bench change things? Yes, for the people who sit there.

Just reread our theme text in the light of the parable of the trail: "No one can serve two masters, either they will love the one and hate the other…." (Matthew 6:24). You cannot serve both God and money. God is larger than money. That is the point. God is always changing. So are our roads. So are we.

The Thanksgiving Basket and Why I Love to Raise Money

I've been raising money since I was a child. My sister and I colluded to negotiate better prices from the tooth fairy.

I worked in my father's garment factory as a teenager, every day from 4 to 8 p.m. in what some called Lent and others called Advent. We called them the Easter and Christmas shopping season. Remember Sears and Penney's and Easter dresses and suits and the same for the secularist's spelling of Xmas? The garment factory always needed extra help in their preseason shipping to the stores. I made good money, making four copies of each receipt for the size 2s through 18s.

I also knew what it meant to be the recipient of the church's (one time a year) Thanksgiving basket. My sister and I always grabbed it off the stoop the second it came. I never wanted to live without money. Poor was bad enough, but people knowing you as poor was even worse. Plus, the people who delivered always snuck up and snuck away, with something like a grin on their now self-validated faces.

While I am quite sure the Matthew 6:24 text is right that money is often God, I am less certain that the binary about serving both God and Mammon is fully correct. I do think it deserves constant reinterpretation, like I tried to do in the last meditation. I think you can serve God by raising money—especially if God is in the driver's seat and money is the gasoline in the tank. No less a guru than Dolly Parton said it this way: "I always wanted enough for me and some to spare." I don't want to put Dolly and Matthew into a debate because I am pretty sure Dolly will win—and, mostly, I prefer Matthew. I also adore Dolly. She is honest. Nobody hates her. She has major common sense. Did you ever notice why everybody loves Dolly? She is without malice. She is funny and uses her sense of humor to gather everybody under the wings of her big boobs. Gestational, generative, generous. Matthew is not that interesting, but he said his piece well too. He just said it as a big binary to bust. She said it as a both/and.

So many people—clergy, especially—love to congratulate themselves on how much they hate to raise money. They clearly imagine that money is dirty and God is clean, that money is bad and God is good. They probably eat purity cereals for breakfast too. And they would vote for Matthew while joining their dreary beloveds in not fully appreciating Dolly. Asked recently about her spirituality, Dolly replied, "It's everything I do." She also said that God is more interested in what we do with 100 percent of our money than 10 percent. Like most of my ideas, I steal my best ones.

I am learning so much from queer theology that I almost feel like I must go back to seminary. Queer theology distrusts every binary—those about boys and girls and those about good and bad and those about Spirit and body. God, who incarnated in Jesus, the word become flesh, likes bodies. God therefore also likes money. Money is one of God's tools, like chocolate or corn flakes made by capitalists.

There is nothing that can be outside of God's world. God cannot be God if there are separate realms. I mistrust people who tell me not to bring politics into the pulpit. How else could politics become good or, even better, holy? Is God exempt from Congress or unconnected to Congress? If so, what happens to old people when they get sick? Do we just pray for them? "Thoughts and prayers" is more than an overused concept that you cannot take to the bank. If I were on God's team, I'd take God to Congress and make sure seniors had money to pay for their health care. I'd take God to Congress and support our politicians to be the very best leaders and caretakers, the ones we desperately need.

Once you escape the binary of texts like Matthew's Mammon, where do you go? Can you imagine a more nested world where even money (idolatrous as it can be) serves God's purposes? Can you imagine loving money so much that you wanted it to be Godly—and you wanted poor kids to have enough of it to withstand the shame in the shaming and blaming of poverty?

One of the places you go is to the man/God of Jesus. You go to his word held by flesh. You say, "*Encarnación,* chili con Christ." You put things together while idolaters try to tear them apart. You say, "I love to raise money." Raising money raises hope.

We could teach fundraising in seminaries, if we could find enough queer theologians. Ask a question about raising money as part of the ordination process. Why be pure when you can serve God?

The Butcher Block Travelogue

When we married, I had three pieces of furniture, and my husband had one. He had found his in front of the former State Street Fruit Market in New Haven and bribed some friends to help him carry it up to his apartment on Bishop Street. That was forty-two years ago. It weighs about three hundred pounds. It weighed that much then and it weighs that much now.

My furniture consisted of an oak trunk bought in Denver that still houses our holiday ornaments; an antique schoolteacher's desk that holds the dog's medicine, the light bulbs, and a lot of extension cords; and a dry sink that holds fancy dishes we never use. His butcher block and my dry sink dated in many a dining room but never really went "out." We should pay a climate surcharge on the way we bought furniture and hauled it around in our peripatetic life.

Here in our new vernacular, less-Victorian beach house, the block just couldn't live in the same dining room with the dry sink and the antique schoolteacher's desk. The trunk had to go upstairs as well.

The butcher block went with us to Amherst (I don't know how), to Chicago, to Long Island, back to Amherst, back to Chicago, back to Long Island, then to Miami, then back to Amherst, then to Greenwich Village, back to Long Island, and tried to fit into our so-called final address in West Haven, Connecticut.

We met in New Haven and married in Amherst. Our dating life involved a 120-mile round trip, using gas prices around 99 cents per gallon. In these places of courtship and nuptials, we read some of James Joyce's *Finnegan's Wake* together.

It begins in the middle of a sentence, undercapitalized as we were then:

"riverrun, past Eve and Adam's, from swerve of shore to bend of bay, brings us by a commodious vicus of recirculation back to Howth Castle and Environs.... "

I think they walked. I don't know much about their baggage or furniture.

In our new house on the bluff in West Haven, the butcher block sadly didn't fit. It didn't get along with the carbon accomplices that had also made the journey with us in various U-Hauls and every now and then in a higher-class form of transportation, like a moving van, with proper blankets.

Truth be told, it never really fit, as no one ever butchered anything on it. It was often the home of large gladiolus bouquets in the summer and beach grasses in the winter. It started its life as functional and ended it as decorative.

At its final circle it decorated the street outside our front window. For three days. At breakfast, lunch, and dinner, our personal résumé of privilege, we discussed its fate. Should we try to sell it? Won't someone just take it? What if they knew its cosmopolitan biography? Or carbon sins?

One morning, we planned to haul it back into the garage. For safekeeping, in case the climate disaster abated. We had bought high over the Sound just in case it didn't.

Garages may be as much accomplices in climate threats due to their love affair with the automobile, but at least they don't buy gas. Garages charge much less than storage units, and that is their virtue.

That morning, we were going to rescue the block from an embarrassing orphanage in West Haven, after such a good if useless life everywhere else. We tried to get it picked up by the thrift shops in order to repent a modicum of our carbon sins but finally realized no one wanted it. Too heavy. Too useless. Too old.

This morning, we took the hand truck up to the street. We looked and looked. It was gone. Someone had adopted it. God bless it on its ecologically sound way. My fantasy is that a local butcher used a horse and buggy to lift it back to his store, where he carves grass-fed beef and free-range chickens on it.

Did I tell you that the butcher block was free and that its transport and care probably cost very little as well? Here, I properly thank it for its service.

May we all treat our furniture, furnishings, stuff with great respect. I know things won't make us truly happy, but they sure are fun while they last.

9

Bricks and Mortals: Holy Uses of Sacred Sites

When the Notre Dame cathedral in Paris burned down, the French were presented with an exquisitely interesting problem. Many Parisians, including the most secular and the most religious, felt like a scar had been made on the sky. They spoke of it often. When will the scar on the sky heal? A lot of people don't have much use for religion but love the buildings religion gives us.

The French had a first significant conversation about whether to preserve the building or build anew. Preservation won. It is not just like it was before the fire, but more so. Clean inside. Delicately ornate. A healed scar. Proposals were made by architects around the world for changes; some even included a revolving rooftop café. Money was hardly a consideration. The center had to hold.

The second interesting conversation around Notre Dame was whether to charge admission. They never had before. The great cathedral was open to all who came. The cost of providing hospitality to a post-congregation church, one where Mass was still held but only for a fraction of the total time the building was open, was enormous in security, cleaning, repair, and hosting. Many thought it would be reasonable to charge the millions of tourists a small entrance fee. They walked through, gaping at a religion they likely did not observe, wondering what religion was/is. If it is a museum, let it act like a museum. Others were horrified. What if a poor person wanted to come in and sit, maybe even pray? This argument felt that admission charges sullied the Spirit of the building. People came up with great compromises: let the admission charges rebuild the many churches throughout France that were dying from deferred maintenance. Again, preservation won. And the false binary did too.

The great cathedral at Chartres also had a major renovation. The windows have been brought out and put back in—to be cleaned. They were "filthy" from decades of candles being lit in the great nave by people, mostly tourists, who visited the marvelous space and had a mini-religious experience in the lighting of a candle. The current priest in charge has refused to replace the real candles with electronic candles—so the renovation will have to be done again in a few hundred years. Or so I hear on the grapevine.

Unfortunately, this is only one of two "religious" interventions in the great religious space. The other is the messaging of *lumières retrouvées*, or light reborn or recovered or refound. The translations matter. *Lumières* means light—and Chartres twelfth- and thirteenth-century builders thought that God was light, and they built the Thomist cathedral around geometric principles that yielded maximal light, flying buttresses and all. The buttresses hold up the larger walls. Before the buttresses, the walls were just too small for windows.

Retrouvez might mean at least "reborn," giving the cathedral some religious oomph going forward. It might also mean—to the preservationist who are doing the work and paying for the work—"recovered" or "refound." You could argue that the cathedral renovation is being done by people who are "preservationists but not religious," in my personal mimic of that phrase about being spiritual but not religious. Or they could be called "aesthetic but not religious."

I am not one bit bothered that so many people care about this great building so much that they are spending extraordinary time, energy, and money to restore it. It is worthy. I am a bit bothered by the lack of God language in the restoration. Has the building been desacralized? Or resacralized? What does this lightweight spirituality mean to those of us currently trying to hang on to our buildings or restore them? Must we also depend on minimalist religion or lost religion?

I'm as good a pagan as anyone and appreciate light as a marvelous metaphor for the Divine. It is also a diminishment, like Church of the Valley, River Church, and other natural replacements for dead dogmatic titles, like First Congregational or First Presbyterian. Nature is great; culture is great. Both together are marvelous religious and spiritual experiences.

We overcultured versions of faith know that we are old and that our sons and daughters don't follow our ways. Thank you, Samuel, at Ramah. But what great space houses a minimalist religious experience—instead of finding a way to find a *new* religious experience? I'd so much rather be reborn than recovered.

I've been employed by religious institutions for fifty-three years. The number of ways we are supposed to keep churches pure and unsullied by money is astounding. Don't charge too much for a baptism or a wedding. Sacre-religious. Phony religious. Impure. The soul is pure; the building is not.

Religion is not the only institution undergoing large changes. Banks will tell you they don't need their buildings either. Likewise, shopping malls and office buildings. Many high schools would give a lot not to look so much like prisons. These changes are about both the building and its purpose at the same time.

One point of entry into Religion 201 is to enter through the metaphors of our buildings and their furniture. This is the incarnational door, the one where we understand the word becoming flesh and "dwelling" among us, as we dwell with it. You can also describe this incarnational door as institutional, the place of infrastructure, the place we sit whether it is comfortable or functional or not. Starting with an intervention into physical space does not demean spiritual or functional space so much as make a choice. Let's go in through the institutional door, the place where people think that when they go to church they are going to a building with an address.

Judson Model

For most of my years in ministry, I have seen church buildings threatening ministries. You could describe that threat another way: We don't have enough money to preserve the container for the holy. The toilet is broken. Some member of the board of trustees says, "I know a guy." That guy, someone's cousin first removed, "fixes" the toilet only to need another cousin to come in about a year. We didn't have enough money for that either.

When I first got to Judson Memorial Church (American Baptist and UCC in Greenwich Village) as senior minister in 2005, the custodian told me that eleven of the twelve toilets in the main building were broken. I said, "Break the last one." That way we'd run out of excuses not to get new bathrooms. The desperation worked. We raised the money and fixed all the bathrooms. We did not use somebody's cousin but took the estimate that was most rather than least expensive.

The legacy congregation of seventy-five or so stalwarts at Judson was tired of both toilets and timidity. *And* they were still willing to take risks on behalf of their future. They believed they had a future and spent money and energy to prepare for it. They knew they had to stop deferring maintenance but also felt their grungy state of disrepair was more honoring the Divine than repairs would be. They were living in a double bind.

Still, the Judson building had outgrown its congregation's capacity to defer maintenance any longer. (Most congregations today—even the big and rich ones—face this dilemma.) Their roof leaked, the organ had burned, the lift was broken. New York University had already taken over a third of the building, in a hostile act, declaring it a firetrap, which it was. NYU paid $3.5 million for the building, leased some of it back to Judson, and put a law school on top of our firetrap. That firetrap had been thirteen apartments, which made possible the youthful excitement of the place. When it was gone, people thought the energy was gone. It wasn't.

It was bloodied but unbowed. The congregation worships on the second floor. Parts could no longer be found to fix the lift. The congregation had done what a lot of congregations do: taken the lowest price for an essential piece of equipment. The elevator was a sturdy lift but could only carry two persons. Instead, it carried cases and cases of water and wine upstairs for years for what was the nonstop party enjoyed in the last century. The lift finally just said "enough." The congregation had begun to worry that the liftlessness might be a metaphor for them, spiritually, as well.

They suffered from a unique combination of imposter syndrome and the curse of fabulousness. They were no longer what they were.

Founded in 1895, alongside the uptown Riverside Church, the American Baptist Congregation had early attracted the funding of John D. Rockefeller, a Baptist who wanted to do something splendid for Baptists. The architect Stanford White was commissioned to plan the building; the stained-glass artist John La Farge created the windows. The marble came from Italy. Greenwich Village changed and changed and now has changed again. Judson was the home of postmodern dance and removed its pews in 1959 to accommodate the dancers: "We had more people on Saturday nights than on Sunday mornings." Many famous artists lived in the former firetrap. The pastor of thirty-five years, from 1960 to 1995, Reverend Howard Moody, was famous for not wanting to spend money on the building, like most of us then. "Feed the poor, not the marble," he said. He also created Clergy Consultation, which created *Roe v. Wade*. He turned the congregation to the great suffering of AIDS. He defended nudity in dancing and other kinds of arts. The Red Berets were founded there. He published regularly in *The Village Voice*. He concluded his services with this benediction: "The Real Service starts now." Before him, Margaret Sanger had stood on the front steps in 1925 and read a letter to the New York State Attorney General that "we will be distributing birth control pills here tomorrow."

The legacy was large for the icon, known as the Judson Church.

New York University was never an honest neighbor. When I first visited John Sexton, the president of NYU, I remembered the plans the university had made in 1924. The map around Washington Square Park showed no Judson. It was all NYU. That was the plan. They were never quiet about it. We were always threatened. They did the hostile takeover for one-third of our property in the 1990s, right after the thirty-five-year tenure of Reverend Moody completed. When I visited with President Sexton, who became a friend, he asked how the congregation was doing. I lied and said, "Marvelously." He responded, "Oh, damn."

We thought in 1995 that our time and place were over. We had "completed." That nagging worry turned Easter by two interacting methods for ministry. One was a community ministry program; the other was hyperuse of the sacred space we did have.

The community ministry happened like this. I said to our then moderator that I needed *somebody* to help me. We had a part-time pianist who was smoking dope in the archive room. We fired her. We had a part-time "administrator" who answered the phone when she felt like it. We fired her too. I told my boss I needed *somebody*. The moderator, Peggy Halsey, said, "Yes!" I advertised at all the seminaries in NYC for an intern. We got seven applications. I said to Peggy, "Wow, these applicants are all so good, I want to hire all of them." She said, "Let's do it. I think we have $35 thousand in an emergency fund somewhere. Go ahead." Spending money is a great idea. Good leaders often have that idea. Scared leaders don't.

We hired the seven students, who were remarkably gifted as filmmakers, community organizers, second businesspeople, and wannabe clergy. Many were gay before they were queer, well tattooed, well-spoken, and young enough to embrace lost causes. They adorned the place by being "youthful" when NYU students or other younger people came around. Because the congregation put its own dollars as front money for its future, we were able to get foundation funding for fourteen years to continue the program. Group supervision on Friday afternoons helped each student identify one project in the wide world of outreach. Their titles were "community ministers." We used the term *teaching congregation* to assure the elders that they were useful. Two elders from the congregation taught the class with me, and dozens of members participated irregularly. In that mutual mentoring, elders joined students in intergenerational experiential learning. Each student had a mentor from the congregation. In about five years, the congregation tipped to membership under forty years of age. In the second five-year period, it tipped to a board of directors with people under forty too. Worship attendance went from averaging 60 to about 200 per week. We admit we purchased the "youth." Over my fifteen-year stint as pastor, we ordained 73 students and graduated 123 community ministers. Year by year the program got better, attracting gifted students from the entire Northeast. Some called it being "Schaperized" or "Judsonized." Others called it learning how to do public ministry from and with a parish base. I called it the arts and crafts of spiritual nurture for public capacity. Still others called it résumé building.

Our students are very much in demand as professional clergy. One of them is now senior minister after my rewirement. Another stayed for five years as our associate and was then promoted to minister. Old and young shared power increasingly in the intergenerational congregation. Often, when younger people enter, older people leave. Here we flipped that script.

These two methods of mutual mentoring and hyperactive use of sacred space shook hands until Covid-19 arrived. We ran out of time and money. The elevator still doesn't work. But the narrative of liftless turned to uplifted.

Before Covid-19, five congregations worshipped in the same building: one Jewish, one queer people of color, one called Home for Harm Reduction for people using drugs, one known as the Muslim Community Center, and the legacy congregation of mostly white folk, affiliated with the American Baptists and the United Church of Christ. (The UCC came in during a financial draught in 1953 and brought the energy of gay friendliness as well as some emergency funding.)

At the peak of the transitional operation, three thousand immigrants per month were receiving legal care at the offices of the New York City New Sanctuary Movement. Foundations paid the rent. Every hallway and closet was filled with trained volunteers helping people about to be detained or deported. Wednesday mornings, people who wanted to dance sober danced from 8 to 10 a.m. in the sanctuary. They called themselves "morning glories." Postmodern dance always had Monday nights. (In a previous renovation in the 1990s, the congregation built a first-class sprung floor for dancing.) Removing those pews, long ago, created a fluidity for preservation of the place and shouted, "This sacred place is a church plus!"

A soup kitchen called Bailout Theater started in 2008. It served excellent food to the houseless and the wider community on Wednesday nights and engaged artists from all over New York. Restaurants contributed the food. We had "Dinner and a Show," anchored by those called homeless. They called the Bailout their spiritual and material home.

Judson did put on a brand-new roof, made of Italian red tile, not shingle, as it had done the three previous times the roof failed. The sight of that tile, from the North and East Side of Washington Square Park, is a marvel. Doing the expensive thing was thrilling for the entire community and congregation. It manifested hope. Just last year the La Farge representational windows were matched by "modern saints." Stanford White would be proud to see what he built "hold up."

During this time our biggest fight was from older "gay" members who objected to the word *queer*. Our biggest joy was changing the nature of our benediction. We continued to blend the sacred and the spiritual. One Easter a nude Haitian dancer performed to much joy and much dismay. Judson will always be trying to outdo itself in edginess. The benediction became, "This service ends here and the next service starts outside." Howard Moody strongly believed that the most important people were outside the church walls. We believed that both the insiders and the outsiders were important. We tried to break false binaries, thanks to Queer theology, about us and them, spiritual and sacred, old and young.

The adaptive reuse of the sacred space brought in the money; the community ministers brought in the juice. Judson lived to pray another day, another way. It was a melody of body and Spirit.

Then Came Bricks and Mortals

The city-wide organization "Bricks and Mortals" was started at Judson in 2018, when we realized that our New York experience was not just ours. Gentrifying developers joined NYU in wanting the land of weakened religious institutions. This mission-inconsistent adaptation of sacred space was not for us. We organized. Many of the congregations and seminaries in New York had become woman run. We had a women leaders' group where we often discussed what it was like to be brought in to wash the dishes.

Our slogan was to live to pray another day another way. We both highly regard the power of church as spiritual home and highly regard the needs of the community. Inside and outside is a both/and, not an either/or. The community needs the church, which needs the community. The theology remained a unique blend of secular and sacred. It also said out loud that Jesus is great *and* not the only way to God. The theology invites the resident congregation to give up its power in a kenotic, self-emptying, gracious act of disposal of itself to its community. This emptying made Jesus look good, while paying the bills. It queered its narrative to material loves spiritual loves material and back.

"Bricks and Mortals" came out of the experience at Judson and then joined dozens of similar experiments throughout the nation. Today there are at least thirty versions of the New York experiment around the country, many transitioning "dead" religious spaces to affordable housing and other adaptive reuses. We meet every other week as faith and finance professionals. Bricks and Mortals continues as a dues-based, New York–based organization. It started with a grant from the New York Community Foundation and the Trinity Churches and continued with a grant from the Lilly Endowment.

Deferred maintenance joins declining memberships in many sites to require adaptation. "Nothing" is always a possible course of action; inaction is also action. As baseball historians say, "Obsolescence is a choice." You can choose to get stiff and stuck and then you steal the church from your grandchildren and go out of business. Or you can mutually mentor and preserve and excite sacred space. The best choice is to blend body and Spirit, God and Mammon, and have them become strong partners in sacred spaces.

Removing the Pews as Metaphor and a Physical Removal

New religion will enjoy new furniture—and new furniture will enjoy new religion. The day of the dining room and the "master" bedroom is also over. Buildings and their furniture are constantly changing. New spaces create new content, and vice versa. What content are we creating by keeping our buildings the same as religion changes? How have our spirituality and theology changed in the last two years? Have they changed?

Why or why not? Punishmentalists have taken over most of religion. You can still find a little grace in some places, but for the most part religion is bypassed as a fuzzy "something" because people don't like being blamed and shamed. The preacher is most frequently imagined as someone shaking their finger at shamed people in pews.

Since pews are a metaphor and an object, they are saying something to people. What is it that they are saying that promotes emerging revelation? What doesn't?

Many people have an urgency for permanence as a plank to eternity or "life after death." Immortality imagines that we can sit still, stay still, build a building, and have it always be the same. Pews are an invitation to sit, stably, and be quiet for a minute. Pews are the opposite of work. They may be intentionally uncomfortable—because most fuddy-duddy, rigid religion doesn't really want people to get too comfortable. Removing the pews is a spiritual act that opens us to new ways of looking at the God/man Jesus, the blended man Jesus, the relationship of this world and the next. It empties the space of rigidity. It is kind of exciting to imagine Spirit joining Space and letting us see anew. We might even be comfortable that way.

Bricks and Mortals acted as consultant on the project in Newport, Rhode Island, that removed 1,200 pews and their dusty cushions, the kind that made folks sneeze when they sat on them. The sanctuary now houses the John La Farge Society. The three-story-high La Farge windows are not representational, like the ones at Judson. They are geometric. They are stunning against the open space in the sanctuary. The heavy furniture around the altar was also removed. The empty space imagines another picture of immortality, one that is light, airy, sunny, and open. That picture is less compatible with hard work, discomfort, shame-and-blame non-participatory religious experience, and a preacher telling you what to think. It might even give capitalism a run for its money. It practices a different Spirit.

In *The Gift*, by Lewis Hyde, we see an analysis of why being good with money is good for you and good for others. Churches find their alleged purity in being part of the gift economy rather than the get economy. False Binary 201 tells you not to get too cozy with impurity.

It is the cardinal difference between gift and commodity exchange that a gift establishes a feeling-bond between two people, while the sale of a commodity leaves no necessary connection. I go into a hardware store, pay the man for a hacksaw blade and walk out. I may never see him again. The disconnectedness is, in fact, a virtue of the commodity mode. We don't want to be bothered. If the clerk always wants to chat about the family, I'll shop elsewhere. I just want a hacksaw blade.

But a gift makes a connection. To take the simplest of examples, the French anthropologist Claude Lévi-Strauss tells of a seemingly trivial ceremony he has often seen accompany a meal in cheap restaurants in the South of France. The patrons sit at a long, communal table, and each finds before his plate a modest bottle of wine. Before the meal begins, a man will pour his wine *not* into his own glass but into his neighbor's. And his neighbor will return the gesture, filling the first man's empty glass. In an economic sense, nothing has happened. No one has any more wine than he did to begin with. But society has appeared where there was none before. The French customarily tend to ignore people whom they do not know, but in these little restaurants, strangers find themselves placed in close relationship for an hour or more. "A conflict exists," says Lévi-Strauss, "not very keen to be sure, but real enough and sufficient to create a state of tension between the norm of privacy and the fact of community. ... This is the fleeting, but difficult situation resolved by the exchange of wine. It is an assertion of good grace which does away with the mutual uncertainty."

In most religious observances, wine and bread are exchanged. There is no bill presented after you eat. Food is understood to be a gift, one to the other. That economy of gift is fundamentally challenging to capitalism. Capitalism, if it stayed in its lane and was part of life and not all of life, might just be fine. Since it tries to take over religious space (churches cannot harbor immigrants?), we need to reimagine religious space as an anchor institution with an alternative and potentially complementary ally to capitalism. We especially need to guard against idolatry, with only one system acting as though it were God. We need to open the space as an object lesson in keeping all space—and ideas—open to consideration.

10

Reparations Are a Holy, Self-Directed Use of Misdirected Money

Reparations in General

There has been a lot of confusion about what reparations are and what they are not. According to the United Nations, reparations include five key components: Cessation/Assurance of Non-Repetition, Restitution and Repatriation, Compensation, Satisfaction, and Rehabilitation. Reparations are a concept rooted in international law that involves specific forms of repair to specific individuals, groups of people, or nations for specific harms they have experienced in violation of their human rights.

Broadly, people usually include the right to eat as a human right because what good are civil liberties if you are starving to death? Hunger is a harm. Thirst is a harm. Having to repatriate is a harm. These harms are not ordinary. They are forms of theft, one over the other.

In 2014, Ta-Nehisi Coates's article "The Case for Reparations" went viral. It was mostly interested in reparations for the American enslavement of Africans, while acknowledging that there is a multitude of violations for which to repent. Americans do not have a corner on this market.

Evanston, Illinois, led the passage of the first tax-funded reparations bill for Black Americans. In California, the conversation continues about reparations for Japanese Americans. Significant progress has been made. In Boston, Massachusetts, a vigorous debate has ended in a long-term agenda for repair.

Sometimes called "The Atonement Agenda," the movement for reparations waxes and wanes in American history and was particularly energized during the time after the George Floyd murder and the many others that followed. Many had also proceeded, but this movement took the slogan "Name the Names" to heart.

Other times called the Intergenerational Wealth Gap, the movement to stop and repent, restore and reconnect, compensate, satisfy and rehabilitate takes many forms. It is a large movement in the matter and spirit conversation, and so large that it is beyond the scope of my inquiry here.

I am particularly fond of an organization that calls itself CTTT, *Come to the Table*, which works especially with people who have generational wealth that began with slaveholding. I am amazed to count four of my good friends in this category. I am particularly fond of their language for reparations that is "restorative justice." There are so many superb organizations at work in this area that it would be foolish to act comprehensive.

What is important to say is that reparations have a long history that has yet to become ordinary. It remains a gleam in our eyes.

Few argue that reparations should *not* be done. The Pew Research Center makes some good points. That being acknowledged, we *do* argue about how to do them. Should they be taxed-based? Voluntary? Both? Should they be government mandated, the way a government might ban all plastic if it wanted to do so? Should they go to individuals or to systems, like entrepreneurial businesses or school systems or free tuition to colleges? Should they be cash gifts or reduced school loans? What might change the ratio of Black wealth to white wealth? Should they be cash gifts to all children at birth, money they could invest over time to right the wrongs on an uneven playing field?

Wiser minds than mine have debated and not yet come to a consensus about how to right the wrongs. It is possible that some wrongs cannot be righted, that righteousness itself is a dream and fairness an overly expensive hope.

Forgiveness, under these circumstances, is impossible. You cannot be forgiven for a mistake or sin or crime you don't stop doing. It is also hard for generations after to take responsibility for what generations before did. "It's not *my* fault," we correctly say. "I didn't do it."

Still, and nevertheless, those of us who take advantage from the systemic ways that give others disadvantage must find repentance on our own. We can join in communities like CTTT or legislate activities like those in many states. We can also offer our individual wealth to acts of retribution. That is my choice, and I know it is a little drop in a big bucket.

If I thought my advocacy for a national restorative justice taxation would work, I'd carry that bucket around. I am too much of a realist for the obvious solution, so I go to my personal bucket and at least use it.

My Drop in the Bucket

As I have hinted at before, my husband of forty-two years and I started out with a little and ended up with a lot. We have semiretired (we call it rewired) with a lot and counting in the bank. Real estate, pensions, markets made us "millionaires" several times over. We grew up in the right decades. We can easily live on that money and have a very nice lifestyle. When we die, most of our nuts will remain untouched, thanks to the capitalism I have been critically and appreciatively discussing.

We have three well-educated children in their early forties, whose education we paid for at private colleges, who make good salaries, and who have children of their own to educate. We helped buy each of them a house when they were in their thirties. They are likely at the beginning of interesting careers and businesses. They don't need our money anymore. (Unless current conditions deteriorate.)

My husband has not agreed to my proposal to enact reparations, so I am only looking at half of our money as a tool to do what I want to do. I'm not saying he will not agree to it, or slightly agree to it, or whatever. Likewise, we have only discussed it with two of our children, and they didn't comment one way or another. All three are seriously antiracist in their perspective and fully understand the argument in the five stages of reparation. We are at the stage of looking at the right way to relieve ourselves of our money and have found several very interesting organizations with whom to work. We will continue to look for a strong tax on the wealthiest and drop our drops into the bucket of some organization like CTTT.

This discussion will be ongoing and only needs a decision in our revised will. Our lawyer understands. Our children understand. We understand.

The vehicle may take some time to discover. Worst case, we will give cash gifts to a dozen families, maybe even our own, if they get in trouble. Or to our grandchildren's education plus somebody else's grandchildren's education.

Our objective is to find the right vehicle. We have no illusions about getting this completely right. Reparation is almost impossible to do with any degree of perfection. There's not enough money in the world to right the wrongs. The challenge is too large, the money amount too small. Plus, white saviorism leaves a bad taste in our mouths.

What we want most to do is to acknowledge and demonstrate with our peers. We want to model in an aesthetic as well as moral way. We know we are not "fixers." We know God is also not a repairman (or woman).

The way we got "a lot" was through systems that prohibited others from doing so. The very years of our active working life were just plain lucky. The years 1965–2020 were a gobble for the already secure. Real estate decisions always worked for us. They don't work for others. Our educations were mostly by scholarship. Not everyone gets a scholarship. We have yet to be the victims of ecological catastrophe. Our own children are looking at mortgage financing rates that boggle the mind. We are moral imperfectionists.

I won't call this dirty money because I don't think money is dirty. That is part of the problem I meditate upon here. We have done some very good things with our money. We have tithed it. We have jumpstarted our children in real estate. The point is that money is misused when it is unevenly distributed. And it surely is. For reasons of luck and coincidence, we made out like bandits. We are bandits. We are bandits because we have taken much from others, without even knowing we were doing it. Unintentional indeed. But harm nevertheless.

Reparations will go a little way to change the overall system where the few have too much and the many have too little. My action, and what I hope to be our action, is parabolic. I want skin in the game of changing the game. I don't hate the players. I do hate the game.

There are other forms of reparation that don't involve having to have money. I think of one of my friend's daily social media habits, which I try to imitate. She promotes other people. She promotes young artists. She tells stories about people trying to start their own business. She tags one or two people every day and sends out the good news of who they are and what they have done to her eight thousand followers on Facebook. Imagine a dedication to the opposite of self-promotion.

Or I think of the international movements of the global culture of repair. In San Miguel de Allende, where we go in the winter, the Tikkun Center joins a global culture of repair. Its slow reforestation of a near desert in the mountains is a prelude to being able to plant crops again here. It teaches schoolteachers to teach school children how to plant trees. The local community foundations buy the trees and the locals plant them. During Covid-19 the Tikkun Center fed two hundred people per day from crops it had begun to grow. It is restoring the reservoir. Its compost piles are beautiful and sprout full-sized papayas; its two hundred chickens walk around and help the schoolchildren shake the grasshoppers out of trees, so they don't destroy the trees. The chickens eat the grasshoppers off the ground. It is more like a parade than an agricultural process. They don't claim to know how to reforest the desert or how to stop the desert. They experiment, using everything the natives and the universities know. They enjoy a deep gladness at this reparation.

In the United States, there are similar large and small organizations. Accion comes to mind. Likewise, Habitat for Humanity, B Corps, Center for Neighborhood Technology. So many people are braced against the wind—and creating beautiful pictures of what life might be like for all!

There are thousands of these permaculture sites, kibbutz-type sites, collective environmental repairing projects around the world. I'd like to live in one of them and join the grasshopper parades.

I also love to sweep my own street. The neighbors come out and join me. We all pick up the litter that people leave behind.

Obviously, there is activism on behalf of public forms of reparation that will do a lot more than my bucket's drop or my broom. Check out Professor Ihsaya Husein at the University of Texas in Austin. She argues that we should ask for higher wages for social-impact businesses. Why not value our work? Doesn't value repair the way we think which might repair the way we act? Why even have a word like not for profit? Isn't there profit in educating people, caring for them, burying them, entertaining them, changing their diapers in nursing homes? Who ever said it was a good idea for hospitals to make a profit or for entertainers to make one? Who did that help? Turning hospitals back into so-called not for profits would go a long way towards mitigating the wealth gap. Sickness should not cause people to go broke, which it does, under the current systems. Yes, hospitals began as religious organizations, from the gift economy. It is a crime what St. Elizabeth's and St. Mary's and Presbyterian and Baptist Hospitals have become. A crime.

We can also ask reparative questions. Reparations work is not just for people who have a lot of money, although we might lead the pack. Obviously, a direct approach would be smartest. Taxing the rich a lot on everything over $1 million a year and using that money to repair the intergenerational wealth gap would be an enormous blessing to them, to the poor, to the earth, and therefore to our culture. That at least would be a splash in the bucket of injury.

I probably overmention one of my parishioners who insisted that he was a self-made man. I knew he inherited his used car business from his father. As his pastor, I needed to repair his self-image. It was actively hurting others because it invoked a kind of shame, unintentionally. Why couldn't they make a dime? Or advance at work? It wasn't helping him, either. He was living adjacent to truth. Being a little truthful is helpful. Over time, he slowly got it. But the myth was so buried in his being that he really couldn't change much.

Andrés Segovia, the great classical guitarist, was given his first guitar. The man who gave him his own splendid instrument told him to pay him back in music, not money. Segovia did not understand. "I could never receive this gift from you. Over time, I promise I will pay you back." The donor said, "You don't understand, do you? All of economy is gift. You can't pay me back *except* with music." Eventually, Segovia understood.

Famous preacher Howard Thurman had a scholarship to college. He didn't have the money for the train to get there. On his way, he met a man who completed his fare. That's how that great man got to be educated to his greatness. The donor was a railroad man—what a great investment he made.

There is music in reparations. There is melody between body and spirit in reparations and restorative justice. The whole of economy is gift. Gift is not just for the deserving, or the self-made. Gift is gift.

The Case of the Missing Check

A lot of people must wonder what happened to their check. Forty acres and a mule? One of the African kids at the first COP (Conference of the Parties; the UN climate conferences that have not yet met their promise) wore a sign around his neck, "Show Me the Money." He was the most photographed person at the meeting. He had made his case very clear.

He was missing his check. The check would not just help him; it would help us all. Climate knows no national borders.

I learned a little something about missing checks a while back. I wrote a story to confess my sins to the donor. The story and the donor's response gave me insight into what it must mean not to be receiving reparations and to wonder why nobody has thought of doing them for and with you. Spoiler alert: it involves his giving me a second gift, one of forgiveness.

Here is the story, which went as an email to the donor:

Whenever someone offers you a check and says put it in your back pocket, at a brunch table, refuse. You are 94.2% likely to remember that it is in the back pocket of your blue corduroy skinny jeans and 5.8% likely to forget.

During the holiday season, some days you go from one brunch to a cocktail hour to a dinner party. You make clam chowder to bring to the brunch and your husband makes a modified Portuguese Fish Stew for supper. There are six at the brunch table and six at the dinner table.

The aforementioned check, clearly on its way to being lost in a pocket that was out having fun, was the occasion of the brunch. The check was given by a new friend of our congregation, who wants to remember the joys of his summers in Little Compton, Rhode Island, and honor his wife who is no longer this side. The donor and I met at a concert that happened to happen at the congregation in one of those summers.

One thing led to another. The donor and the forgettee met again at a funeral. They met for lunch. The donor lives in New Hampshire where the forgettee often visits. His group home is very close to her friends. She visited his apartment to see the marvel of his grand piano and to hear the eulogy he had given his wife a scant five months earlier. They became friends.

One thing led to another and a fund for the church steeple was established to honor his wife. That's how the check ended up in the pocket after brunch.

At the second meal and party of the day, a new indoor fire had been lit and the scotch had been downed by the men and the vodka by the women, the loser briefly remembered the check was in her pocket. She was sitting at one head of the table, on the south side of the Westport River in a very small cottage, one already strained by the six people who were eating there. Quite a bit of the kitchen had already been stored in the bedroom. She carefully put down her glass and put the check directly east on the plant table that had the blooming Christmas cactus and five other plants. She made sure the small paper square was attached under the plate that housed the cactus. When she awoke to a kitchen that looked like someone had thrown a large party in it, she went immediately to look for the check and to take such check to the bank or at least to work. She wanted to brag about the donor's generosity and her acuity. She not only loves to raise money; she loves to brag about raising money. She might even love money.

The check was not there. It is still not there as once more, in real time, as I really write this, I just lifted all five pots off their bottoms, usually called liners, and investigated for the ninth time the whereabouts of the missing check. This is the third day since the check disappeared that I have cleaned the entire cottage, vents, lifted all the furniture, and scoured the garbage. Jesus rose on the third day; the check did not.

I did extra yoga and stretching and Pilates and Alexander from my comfy blue mat on the floor later the first day. Having said way too many times, approximately 188 times, "it will turn up," I decided to go into a deeper dive into the mystery. I had already blamed my husband for taking it, and perhaps he did. "I took the garbage out and put all the mussels and clam shells on the top of the bag." I personally had taken the tablecloth off the table and shook it out in the yard. Therein lies my best clue. The check flew off the plant table, slid under the couch or the bureau, and all I needed to do was stretch long enough to look under all those places long enough.

No check.

I gave the matter till Thursday, when I vowed I would step up to my perfidy, drenched as it is in fun and gladness, covered over by the excess of Christmas parties and gratitude for my new friend. I know how generous he is. I heard what he said about his wife. I assumed he would be generous about his generosity.

As Thursday approached, I procrastinated. I called my neighbor and asked if he had by accident picked up the check. Or found it in his front yard. He was on the edge of offended. Bob, a wonderful member of the church, was sitting next to me at dinner Sunday night; he proceeded to tell me a terrible story, after which he told me [he] hadn't seen the check. His father had given him a check one Christmas long ago. He lost it. The father never gave him another chance. Things were worsening.

Anyway, I told David this whole story and introduced it with the above email.

Dear David, attached is the story of the missing check. Please do cancel the check in the odd case that it has fallen into the Westport River down below and a lost sailor found it. Love, Donna.

The Donor's Response to My Email:

I haven't stopped laughing at the humor and the agony embodied in your story. Another suggestion. Perhaps you did give it to the treasurer? I doubt the bank would cash it for a random finder. Nevertheless, I think I'll put a stop payment order in on it as I write another for you when the sun rises tomorrow. Finally, I find it hard to get mad at the situation. Not to worry. I am not Bob's mean father. Love, David.

The poor of the world did not lose the check. We never sent it.

When we acknowledge that we have made bad or impulsive or habituated decisions, we start to do something right in a way that might be contagious. We often make financial decisions—like reparations—that end up costing more than we thought they would. Surprise is a good friend of money.

We found the large, beautifully shaped copper sink on our very first day in Mexico. It showed us the real and lovely expense of money itself. There it was, hanging perpendicular on the wall of a beautiful copper shop. We checked its price immediately, and we were off by about $2,000. The sink cost $900. We didn't buy it till the end of our trip. We searched and searched for another memento of the time because we had a habit of shopping long for just the right object. That sink kept calling our name. We thought we could just carry it on the plane. Nope, we also thought it wouldn't cost much to ship it because it was so light. We also knew that our next-door neighbor was a plumbing genius, and he could do anything.

Eventually, we realized that it would need a special stand. The shipping costs were $240, twice what the store owner assumed. The sink had stayed in its custom-designed box in the garage for quite a while, as we mused about installing it.

We were joking with our friends at dinner about the cost already of the sink. Self-depreciating humor about a rapidly appreciating sink? She knew a person who had a special piece of walnut in a large barn that would be perfect as a platform for the copper sink. Indeed, the sink looked great on her walnut platform, and so for $500 more we bought the slab. Our usual handyman, Angel is his name, said no, this was too big a project for him to cut out. We'd have to go to the only expert in New Haven, a Byelorussian friend of our Ecuadoran handyman. He loved the wood, loved the sink, and charged $1,100 to cut out the hole. I can go on.

The $2,500 Mexican copper sink thrilled our Puerto Rican neighbor, the plumber, and after telling us to be more careful the next time we fall in love with some object, he put a $45 faucet on it and refused to take another nickel. He was pitying us.

When the price goes up on something beautiful, there are at least two ways to feel. One is embarrassed. The other is bemused. We are embarrassed and bemused.

Something in this story reminds me of what Mark Hannah is purported to have said about politics: "There are at least two important things in politics. One is the money, and I can't remember the other."

I've been arguing here for quite a few pages that when we say "it's all about the money" we are violating the covenant between matter and spirit.

Some things are just priceless. Look at all the help we got with the sink. We got to pay a woman in a copper shop in Mexico, a shipper in Mexico, a miller in New Hampshire, a craftsman and a plumber in New Haven. Our sink is downright cosmopolitan. Plus, it is very beautiful, and we get to use it every day. It is a bargain.

Whatever we do to repair the world, we dare not be too attached to even it. Our "legacy" is light. It is small. The world and its cosmos are much larger than the fun we have with our sinks and our sinkholes. Having given my life to church work, it won't surprise you that I am interested in churches and their legacy. It is often hard to know where I stop, and they start.

I am also well-schooled in the dangers of excessive attachment. One can become much too attached to one's legacy, especially if it involves temples.

The best message for my muddle is in the way Jesus felt about temples, supposedly the greatest of the great human accomplishments.

Jesus had a very complex relationship to the meaning of temples. Some say that he even got crucified precisely because of what he said about the temple: "Destroy this temple and I will raise it up in three days… " (John 2:19). Jesus had a very hard time caring about temples and a very easy time caring about what they were supposed to mean. If they point to God, great. If they point to themselves, not great. The religious authorities and their building committees were not pleased with his riddle.

I may stress out about my money and its uses all I want. But that is likely to topple the temple of where I am to be pointed.

There are multiple other Christian texts that give us this same interesting picture of the relationship of the spirit to the flesh, the bricks to the mortals. You would think they were all written for the fire at Notre Dame Cathedral in Paris. They include, "We are treasures in clay pots" (2 Corinthians 4:17). Treasure indeed, but clay treasures. They won't last. Also, "Your bodies are a living sacrifice" (Romans 2:1). "Your bodies are holy, and they are bodies…." Or "Your body is a temple" (I Corinthians 6:19). Bricks and mortals; bodies and spirits are meant to connect in the right relationship. Their connection is holy. Their disconnection, where one is superior to the other and not mutually servant to the other, is not holy. And together, both spirit and body point to something larger than even their own time and space.

We might gain a kind of faith that has fewer props. We might lose some of our merch on behalf of some of its meaning. There is always great opportunity in great loss. Christians believe that life follows death. Weeping/night; joy/morning. And it is time, way past time, to face into the loss of our temples, the loss of our props, the loss of our sturdiness and our prominence and our security—but not the loss of our religion. Maybe it doesn't worship on Sundays, while sitting in pews, at 11 a.m., but it does worship.

I am not a little bit worried about God. God will be fine. I am very worried about religion. As long as we focus on the insiders and their pews, in our real estate and in our hearts, we will continue to decline and pretty soon all have mis-spelled signs on our front lawns. All are welcome here.

If we pay attention to the props of our faith—as beautiful as they are—we will become a faith of props, not a faith that changes people and affirms them. So, Jesus, with whom I quarrel often because it is so hard to really follow him, is right. We don't really need temples that say *forever* to us. We need temples to be fluid. We don't need to demean temples so much as to change them up. Sometimes we need to feed the souls first and the bodies second. We need to keep body and soul together, bricks and mortals together in a holy, not an unholy or imbalanced, alliance. Many of us turn our houses (and the sinks in them) into props and temples. The human, including me, has a great propensity to try to worship the small thing and ignore the large.

A restored chateau called "Chateau La Coste" in Provence brought me to tears once.[1] It had a "universal" chapel at its hilltop, renovated by Tadao Ando. It also had works of art by Ai Wei Wei, Andy Goldsworthy, and more. It was bought by an Irishman who wanted to marry the local to the artistic.

The chapel was like so many abandoned chapels on the road to Santiago de Compostela in Northwestern Spain: sun-blanched stone, square, small, forgotten. I know my tears came abruptly because so many American church buildings are about to go the same direction. They are about to be forgotten, with the front door ajar and the weeds breaking up the concrete. Very few have the simple beauty of the chapel at La Coste. But all of them have or at least had that connection between the best architecture a little community could afford and the local.

They put together soaring steeples and baked bean suppers. They connected the babies to the old people and did "hatching, matching, and dispatching" for as long as anyone wanted. Then their time gave out. Some combination of secularism, multiple options, soccer on Sundays, two-career families, intermarriage, and conceit put most of our buildings and congregations out of business. Very few will transition to the next decade.

The question driving me is what would happen if we did a creative adaptation as forceful as the one at La Coste? As married as the art and the locale are there?

There, a Japanese architect encased the building in glass. Yup. He built a glass box around the chapel. It looks a little like a chapel on ice. Or a chapel framed.

He also put in three benches and three "holes" in the stone so that outdoor light could come up and light the altar. Moreover, he put in a wooden door that doesn't quite fit the entryway, allowing a sense of the afterlife and heaven to be ever so visible at all times, as you peer out and wonder what's going on in the cockeyed arrangement. People who would "never darken the door of a church" can safely walk outside and around in the glass enclosure, which is maybe 18 inches wide. The spiritual but religious crowd doesn't need to be made uncomfortable by worshipping inside. They can be safely close and also outside of any insults to their religious sincerity. I so love spiritual but not religious people for their refusal to be hypocritical. Some of the conceit that destroyed churches and their buildings came from a strong willingness to be hypocritical.

The chapel at La Coste gives tourists and outdoor museumgoers a spiritual experience. What could our buildings do in their environment to also marry the artistic and the local and the spiritual? Surely, we could remove the pews and have multiple uses for our "sanctuaries."

Outside the chapel at La Coste there is a large, red-beaded plastic cross. It reminds one of a Paris subway station. Or a rosary. Or both.

What does the South of France and a Japanese architect have to say to American churches, all but gone and in hospice?

One is that there is a tremendous opportunity, hidden in plain sight, to reimagine religion and spirit. These buildings can all become luxury apartments or groovy restaurants—or they can even more creatively adapt to their circumstances. They can become something different than they were. Maybe they are coffee shops or low-income housing, or both. Maybe they are work spaces that are stained glass lit for people who need free wi fi. Maybe they are day care centers or elder care drop-in centers. Maybe they are yoga studios, theaters, dance spaces—places for artists that don't cost a fortune. Some of these artists may decide to worship with the remnant congregation on a Sunday afternoon or Saturday evening in a truly flexible space. Maybe they offer free childcare and spaghetti suppers on Friday nights to working families who need a date night, some community, and some fun time but can't afford it.

The congregation in Newport, Rhode Island, removed their pews and gave their John La Farge stained glass windows a whole new audience and light. The chapel at Vassar is becoming a meditation and yoga center. Many worship spaces in New York City are becoming senior or low-income housing—so as to avoid the mission inconsistency of gentrification and its partner, racism.

Almost for sure, they start by removing the pews. Those pews have nothing to do with the flexible spirituality people are seeking today. Pews are props.

Perhaps on Friday nights joining Alcoholics Anonymous and Narcotics Anonymous and all the rest of the anonymous "downstairs" people, there is a place where people who are using opioids can come to pray and be touched and held together by something larger than the chemicals that now bind them. And I do mean bind them. Religion comes from the word *religare*, to bind together. Why bind alone?

On Wednesday mornings at my former church, Judson, we sometimes host "Morning Glories." Two hundred people come to dance, sober, and to enjoy the ecstasy of a strong beat. (I have a beautiful photo of this from *New York Magazine*.)

Before you get on a high horse about people touring religion or tourist religion or sidelined religion or how "awful it is to think of church people being sidelined in their own space," take a good, strong look at what it means to be religious. It may mean precisely to be sidelined. It may mean to think of your clients as those who aren't coming rather than those who have their own personal pew. Our church's slogan is that we are "the perfect place for imperfect people." That's why our growing congregation is dwarfed by the other users of our building, ten to one. Some 2,400 a week walk through our doors;

200 worship together on Sundays. I like that ratio. And from it, our building will creatively adapt. My tears at La Coste were tears of joy, not sorrow.

If that place lasted as long as it did, so may my hopes for accountability and legacy, something a little good left behind.

11

Getting Personal about Money

A Personal Budget

What is the difference between being a servant and being a slave? A servant chooses service; a slave complies with orders. What is the difference between work and play? Repeating, play is anything you want to do and work is anything you have to do. What we choose is important. Choice is important. There is a problem with choice: it is not always possible to choose what we want or do what we want or be who we want.

First, there is the budget. Most people have over 80 percent in set costs at the start of the process. Insurance. Rent. Food. More insurance. Loan repayments. You may choose to do a lot of fun or good things with your money but only have less than 20 percent of what you earn as discretionary. You work hard for the money! Then the money works hard on you.

There are surprises pretty much every month. Our budgets may be brilliant and done with great care—but they are as surprised as we are at the things we forgot to consider. Who can stand remembering that in Connecticut you pay a tax on your car, every year? Probably a good idea, given the roads and storms. That being said, who can remember?

Dentists exist whose voicemail says that serving you is their top priority. Then they forget three times in a row to find out if your insurance takes that drug that fixes your gums. Why? "That's not my job." BTW, the insurance does not pay for the drug the dentist recommends. It costs $224.00 per dose. You have eight pockets, not the kind where you put your keys but the kind that hurts your gums. Four hundred 800 numbers later, you find out that you can get three doses per year. In three years, you'll have a tooth or two left. (Yes, this is the United Church of Christ [UCC] health insurance, Concordia. I get my dental work done in Mexico, where the dose is free and done in a small way after each cleaning. Each cleaning costs a total of $45.)

You may want to play in the afternoon, but you work instead for the insurance company. There is not much more time left to do what you want. When people make up new language called "side gigs," they are talking about the surprises in our careful budgets. Side gigs are also an interruption of our carefully planned lives.

When Jesus and other similar gurus say that the first must be the very last, how does that apply to a broken society and a broken system? It means that we pay attention to how all our money is used. That we become more grateful for what we have, even if it is only an unencumbered percentage.

It also means constantly questioning the systems that hurt all of us, not just some of us. Only the genuinely rich are not enslaved. That is a hard fact and a true one.

The UCC insurance company also turned me down for life insurance, at age seventy-six, after I went back to working full time and became able to get the small benefit again. Why? I had cancer in 2001. If I spent a couple hours a day, assembling the documentation of my original diagnosis and my annual clear mammograms and talking to the 800 numbers, I could get the life insurance benefit. Why did I bother? Because some people might not be like me, with another life insurance to cover me. They might have a robot determining that they didn't deserve the insurance. Note to reader: you only have to go back five years in your health insurance history that you disclose. I didn't know that.

The last don't have to be last, especially if those first in line pay attention to who else is there.

Many people don't make personal budgets because they don't want to know how much they have or don't have. Others use the excuse about surprises. There are so many surprises in personal finance. Why not go with the flow?

What follows is a guide to the numbers you might not want to know but need to know. If you are running an annual deficit, which many people are, you may need to make changes. Or at least become aware that you are going deeply into debt. Ignorance of what you have or don't have is a form of slavery. You are owned by what you don't have. Knowledge is a form of servanthood, first to yourself, then to those you love.

Remember the line from the Lord's Prayer: Forgive us our debts as we forgive our debtors.

Debt is not a crime. It is real for many.

Anyway, here is the best guide (of many excellent ones) for budget making I know. Fill in the blank. Try to understand that there will be surprises. Budget for them. Then they won't hurt as much.

I believe in praying toward every one of these categories as I evaluate their use and continued usefulness to me. I give God thanks for my income and my expenses; my insurances and my food; my electricity, water, oil, and gas. I give God thanks that I am (if I am) able to give 10 percent of my income to my church and other so-called charities, most of which are social change organizations. Likewise, my taxes to my city, county, state, and country. I don't give thanks for my debts because I try to have very few. These debts go to usurious practices, and they give people who already have too much, more. I often repent what debt I have. Debt may not be a crime, but it does double-duty harm to ourselves, and then to others.

Budget Categories

Overall income

    Income _____

    Solar income? _____

    Investment income? _____

    Honoraria, royalties, side gigs _____

Expenses

    Rent or mortgage _____

    Electricity _____

    Internet, cable _____

    Gas _____

    Heat _____

    Water _____

Insurance health _____
Insurance house _____
Insurance car _____
Insurance life _____
Insurance eye _____
Insurance dental _____

Car payment _____
Car maintenance_____
Car gas or electricity_____
Public transportation _____
Car tax _____

Food _____
Clothing _____
Carry around or pocket money, "weekly"_____
Taxes state_____
Taxes municipal _____
Taxes national_____

Tithe, generosities, pledges _____
    (Half to your congregation, other half to everybody else as a recommendation)

Tennis, gym, clubs _____
Vacation(s) _____

Usually, once you pay all these things, you have a decent balance between input and output, income and expenses. Often, you might want to add luxuries or preparations.

Grandchildren gifts to ensure their college education _____
Savings for college tuitions for your own kids _____
Savings for a big birthday or anniversary _____
Savings for house maintenance, like a boiler or a roof _____
Rainy day funds for health crises _____
Savings for a new car _____
Paying down debt you may have accumulated _____

If you discover genuine gaps between essentials and income, you need to imagine a move, a change in work, or both.

Gaps are announcements that change is needed. Balance is the objective. You don't want to be a slave to money—either to what you don't have or what you do have.

If you are surprised by how much you do have, then it is time for the second naiveté of budgeting. You can add more luxuries and more preparation, and that means more stewardship and more servanthood as well as more cruises. Tithing the excess is often a very interesting process.

Choice is the objective in budgeting. Choice is a good way to manage the energy of money. The more you manage it, the less it manages you. When you pause to think and pray and figure out what THEE wants, you do so in order to make that famous melody between body and Spirit.

Refinishing a Chair and Personal Accounting in Our Budget

If you have a good balance between income and expenses, hooray for you.

If you have too little income and too many expenses, so that you have no time for luxuries or planning for surprises, you may make changes in how you spend, live, work, and play. Change is good. Frequent change is very good. Being able to change and look directly at new circumstances, whether promising or threatening, is good. You'll feel much better once you become a realist about your holdings and your earnings.

Many people are in debt over their heads and drowning. It is surprising how many people are able to help people who live or exist while drowning. *Talk to* your *debtors* and your *bank* and *whoever else will listen to you.* You will be surprised at how much help is out there.

Change is often very hard. We need personal accounting, and it takes time. At the end of this book, I will give a hundred-day "program" of prayers, pauses, and meditations to begin to get real and to unmask and come out of hiding about money. For now, consider the behavioral prompts that follow.

The first is the Alexander technique, already mentioned. The second is Refinishing a Chair. The third is personal accounting and accountability.

There is a wonderful spiritual practice called the Alexander technique, which you might want to borrow in budgeting. I've already brought it up as a spiritual practice, but here I'd like to recommend it as an analytical tool for each category in your budget, both under income and expenses.

Alexander says that the best things we can do for our overall posture and well-being is to pause and inhibit our "slouches." There is a wonderful new book called *Slouch*, which argues that our slouches are fears. When we refuse to budget our resources, for whatever reason in whatever way, we slouch into fear.

Alexander is an old technique to stand up straight. It also argues that we learn young to slouch because we are afraid to look straight at things. Instead of yelling at you to stand up straight like our parents used to do, Alexander invites us to stand up straight. Budgeting is about facing and straightening out our resources. They become a service to us, not we to them. Indeed, this method of behavior is about doing less on behalf of more. It is about awareness of how our body is working. How we sit on our butt studs. How we breathe from the bottom, not the anxious top of our diaphragm. How we keep our head on top of our spine. How we often need a midday lie-down just to know what we know and press our feet into the floor and pull our belly button down to the ground. We don't use our torso to move. We move from our expansion and get taller that way.

It is an inhibiting pause to do what we have called here meditate, pray, reflect. It is a bodily assent to material behavior. It is a very useful way to think about budgeting.

Inhibition is understood as the primary control. Inhibition is another kind of prayer, pause, or action-reflection. It gives us permission not to just do what we do or tend to do or feel like doing. Inhibition is when we say "no, thank you" to a behavior that is not helping us.

Another metaphor and practice for meditation about money is to make believe you are a chair and every now and then you need a refinishing or a repainting. You must take yourself down to the wood and allow yourself to be renewed.

When you really need to make a chair new, you must take it down to the wood. You might want to paint it or give it a new finish or coating. When your budget is way out of whack—either with too much or too little—it could be time for a refresh and refinish. Things do wear out. What used to work will not necessarily always work.

There is a trend these days toward distressed furniture, but very few of us want to give the impression of distress. Nobody needs any more of that. We have plenty of unacknowledged maintenance of our roofs and sinks and electrical systems—and are deeply aware in 2025 that we need to make big, not little changes.

Most institutions are having a makeover season as well. We are leaving behind our physical offices and our copy machines. We may be down to one staff member. Recognizing this time of change and a deep need for refinishing, not just for a quick job, we also look at our governments, our environments, our educational systems, our DEI systems, our national debts, and so much more.

We are hardly alone in our makeover. For now, let us be deliberate in taking off the old finishes and giving a good look at the clean chair. Let us give a good farewell to our offices and copy machines. Let us get ready to be new, having done proper grief, and make even more proper choices for the future we can.

Our rooms have changed. Very few of us use the dining room table. Or call the primary bedroom the "master" bedroom. Or use the front door. We can use these changes as ways to look at how our budgets might change. If we have a lot of space we aren't using, we might want to marry form to function in our "interior" decorating as well.

Jesus himself said, "Behold, I make all things new." He was a great refinisher.

We may need to refrain from spending as well as rearrange our spending. We may need to sacrifice our privacy and live again with family or take in a boarder or two. In earlier immigrant experience, people often said, "Hurry up and eat, we need the tablecloth for a sheet." People often lived in three shifts in Greenwich Village. Some may even have been happier. We may also need to be more generous, if we have trouble spending all our money. The point is to make friends with our resources and our debts and our situations. Befriending money is much better than fighting it. That requires realism, not slouching.

Finally, consider personal accountability about your "numbers" to manage your money and time as opposed to letting it manage you. When I had my fiftieth ordination anniversary, many of my older friends advised me to do a personal accounting. I did so.

It follows here.

Basically, I have been a failure while working hard every day.

I have also been richly blessed by thousands of educational and intimate relationships with real live people. My mission was spiritual nurture for public capacity and still is. Ellis, a six-year-old boy, asked, "When is Donna coming back?" a few months after I concluded my last interim. He liked my children's sermons.

If you read what I wrote about temples in the reparations chapter, you will know that I am more than disturbed by the death and hospice of religious institutions.

We have lost at least three generations of access to any religious tradition, no matter how stupidly or rigidly it was taught. We have a vacuum of shared cultural meaning and values that is extraordinary. The empty wells clang as people put their buckets down to get some living water. It's not there. Or, it is there, but it is much further down and inaccessible. I often speak of the Divine as a holy grail, deeply embedded and hidden.

When our offspring tell us they don't want our "stuff," the older generation, like me, also hears the obvious. We don't want your traditions or cultural or spiritual legacy either. They mean little to my own children, much less yours.

You would think with all the effort and all the money and all the relationships and all the legacy, that more would have mattered. What did matter was the constant spiritual nurture for public capacity.

In my life as a pastor, I have raised over $10 million from good people (and foundations) who had money and wanted to do good with it. Many of them inherited their wealth. They wanted to use it well. They wanted a shared glass of wine with the poor. They weren't earning their salvation. They were giving to receive and receiving to give.

One of my best donors ever was a woman who put cardboard in her shoes, like I did when I was a kid. She didn't see the reason to spend money on herself. Another was an alcoholic in recovery whose life was saved in a church basement.

50 Years of Ministry: 474 weddings; 244 funerals; 114 baptisms, 205 students in classes; 9 youth groups; 112 interns; 335 ordinations; 1,594 sermons.

Tucson, Philadelphia, as associate minister, then urban minister, then Yale as associate chaplain.

Amherst, Riverhead, Miami, New York as pastor.

Also, a decade stint as area minister in Western Massachusetts and a three-year stint as executive director of the Urban Academy in Chicago, courtesy of a generous Lilly Endowment grant.

Since rewirement, two interims, three bridges.

In my first parish in 1973 a former police social worker gave her entire inheritance of $254,000 to the Open and Affirming Movement in the United Church of Christ (UCC), which coined the phrase, God Is Still Speaking. That took the UCC into leadership with inclusivity around the LGBTQ+ community. Winifred Johnson was closeted and gay.

In Philadelphia, my next church tabernacle in West Philadelphia, we founded an organization called Women Organized Against Rape. It changed how emergency rooms and police treated women who said they were raped. A private donor, who had been raped and left college because of it, gave the organization $50,000 in startup money. This money meant we could both staff and develop these organizations, which are now in business enjoying the fruits of their labors.

Then at Yale, I have already described the Community Cab Company.

Then in Massachusetts, in my first solo pastorate, given to me by the Massachusetts conference minister who thrust three of us women onto local congregations, I had to "fire" the head of our stewardship committee, who was also the chair of the Business Department at UMass. He was guilt tripping the congregation with his annual message. You should give. You must give. I am going to show everything everybody gives outload. We have a seven gabled roof that was leaking. As soon as he left with a huff, the congregation raised $200,000 to repair most of the roof. They may raise the roof. They might raise the roof. They could raise the roof. Not they must.

Rename words. And you'll find people want to give to get and get to give. They may live!

When I took the call to go to the Coral Gables Congregational Church in the late 1990s, their endowment hovered around $13 million. (*Call* is what clergy call jobs.) In the three months between the time I said yes and they said yes and we said yes, the stock in their endowment doubled. The original donor, a certain Mr. Havinghorst who founded UPS, was no longer managing the money. Whoever was did both well and good. And it didn't hurt that their stock doubled in the move that took the stock public.

The endowment doubled in size from $13 million to $26 million, between the time they offered me the position and the time I came. I knew that such a large endowment would be inimical to their own stewardship and giving. I even had a magical thought that was as true as most magic is: with that much money, they could easily tip into a post-Christian church. Forgetting about Jesus would be much too easy. Thus, I took the job on condition that we spend $1 million per year of it, to reduce the temptations.

They were doing beautiful things with their money. In fact, they were *good* with *money*. They spread it around while maintaining a healthy personal security. They had a balance in being good to themselves and good to others. So many of us want that balance. Still, most of us have to settle with imbalance: we work too hard to please others or the boss or both because we have too little personal security. Or we become rich bastards ourselves—the kind of people who stuff themselves with wealth, imagining they are more deserving and better than the other poor bastards.

Possibly, this appreciation for my soon-to-be flock was the first time I thought about writing a practical and spiritual guide to money.

I thought they had the answer: use money for your personal security on the practical side; then do good with whatever is left. You may even reverse the order and start with the surplus for extravagant good and return to the security. You won't need as much security if you are having fun.

The ancient code of Maimonides agrees. The acts of charity or Tzedakah are a form of justice and personal joy while also starting with self and family and moving up in nine stages of relative goodness. It is a commonsense approach to money: you are to use your income to secure yourself, your family, your neighbors, your friends … going up to a final call to give money away anonymously, so no one knows the good you are doing but you. There are many variations on this theme, but they ascend to goodness and emphasize that giving helps the giver as much as it helps the one who receives the gift.

I was like any poor kid from upstate New York and had replaced my eyeballs with dollar signs as soon as the offer came. Oh, the money I would make. The security I would enjoy. The three kids' college tuitions no longer my next ticket to the poorhouse. And, simultaneously, I knew that a very secure church could make a lot of what John Lewis called "good trouble." I knew the bad money could do and I knew the good it could do. I was interested in both coulds.

If we had that much money, we needed to really work on giving it away, wisely, strategically. We needed to develop partners that could also feel as good as we felt about giving it away.

I signed the contract and covenant as we decided to give away $1 million per year of the endowment. They unanimously agreed in a congregational meeting that had an unfamiliar sense of joy.

Year One, we matched $1 million each from the Annie E. Casey Foundation and the Knight Foundation to get the $3 million it took to start Accion in Miami. Our leverage offered opportunities for all of us in a mutual aid society. Accion was a successful microlending program in many spots on the globe. It had not yet come to the United States. Miami was its trial balloon. The community reinvestment bank law had become very difficult to achieve. As one of Saul Alinsky's first female students, I had been a part of the Community Reinvestment Act passage, which required banks to fund local projects. These microloans were about as local as you could get, going to barbershops and car washes and power washing companies. Accion was doing $13 million in loans per year a few years ago. Our startup has already quadrupled more than once. Imagine how proud our members were to be a member of the church that did that. And P.S.: it increased our membership during the high periods at eighty new folks per month.

Year Two, we endowed $1 million to ten "MacArthur/Miami" grants, at $100,000 per year. We called them the Miami MacArthur Genius awards, and we gave no-strings-attached gifts to ten well-chosen local leaders. Each one of them gave back to their communities for decades, including one Daniella Levine, who went to the Kellogg School of Business to learn governance and is now mayor of Miami–Dade County.

Year Three, the schools in our four zip-coded neighborhood of Coral Gables cut their music departments. Just flat out. No more music in the schools. We created music departments in each of the public schools in each of these zip codes and formed a band at the church, using famous jazz musicians to teach from our own music program. (Yes, before the stock split, the church was already famous for its summer jazz program of stars brought in from around the country.) These people were thrilled to come in and teach local students.) The church also had a band of young people for every fourth Sunday and went on to populate its youth group.

Year Four, the program stopped. There was a mini-recession afoot at that time. The Sunday School wing of the historic building had bad mold. It was time to stop the noble experiment and take care of the endowment and the building. Life has cycles. Common sense understands the cycles and developmental seasons of money.

It was time to return to the expensive self-preservation that money provides. Why expensive? It doesn't bring in young people or a positive pride in belonging to your church. It makes you look like every other church, many of which are in need of a PR firm to correct their selfish, judgmental images. Humans experience joy when they belong to each other, when they are connected to each other. That's why the church in Miami was so happy. It had replaced Spectatoritis with active participation. Its money made money, membership, youthful participation, and more. It would never have earned that much if left unspent. Being good with money is about spending money and spending it out loud and often. Congregations are like people: the more we give away, the more we get.

Accion now makes $12 million a year in profits and reinvests it in small businesses. It has helped over five thousand people create their businesses. My favorite is the washer business. "Because I didn't have to rent a power washer every day, I could work eight hours per day instead of twelve," says a business owner. "That meant I could do homework with my son. I was also able to hire two other people to wash and keep the equipment in use. And my son is doing very well in school." Often, when we talk about leveraging money, we mean just that. Leverage money. We could also talk about leveraging goodness. Leveraging to include family values as opposed to overworking parents. Leveraging that understands that it is the sea that rises to lift the boats, not the boats.

Is Time Money?

The answer is yes. Time is money. We can give more time to making money or less time to making money, depending on what our budget review reveals. Time is much more precious than money and is also different than money. Time runs out, for all of us. Money is a form of energy that lasts.

My 2024 calendar burst its seams, early in the year. I had turned the pages on April and May too often, shoehorning a few more events into the small squares on the page. I had to ask myself why and how I had worn out a perfectly well-made calendar so early in the year. One reason revealed itself like this: I am getting older and didn't want anyone to know so I kept saying yes when I should have said no. Age limits how much we can stuff into time. Some of us take a while to understand that.

You can have what you can let go of, say most spiritual wags. You can't have what you hang on to. Ah.

Money is a form of energy with which we daily interact. Buy the coffee. Work the job. Get the groceries. Eat the food. Give the gift. Assess the cost. Adjust the budget. Pay the rent. Put the tithe in the envelope. Put another bill on automatic payment with your bank.

Decline an invitation to Aruba because you can't afford it this year. Money is never far away in thought or pocket or pocketbook. It rarely gets a good look, a dusting off, a cleansing, or a rededication.

If you go to church, you participate in a weekly "offering." I like to think of all my expenditures as offerings. They are holy. Water and warmth are surely holy. Even my car is holy. God knows I spend enough time in it! Only a certain amount of money is publicly blessed. This meditation takes that liturgical moment and orients it to breakfast, lunch, and dinner. It gives thanks for the ability to give. It says that our tithe is less important than what we do with the other 90 percent. (Thank you, Dolly.)

Money might best be defined as an energy that sustains us, amuses us, and confuses us. It gets way too much attention in its ubiquitous presence. It gets way too little attention in a spiritual way. We may be very grateful to have money, but we don't thank it enough. We take it for "granted."

Even the intention to become more "whimsical" about money takes a minute. We have to give ourselves permission to fluff it up like a pillow or dust it off like an unremarked bureau or desk in a "spare" room. Whimsy is a lightness of being that brings light to what is usually a shadowed situation. Making jokes about your budget, including the unexpected need for two dental insurances, goes a long way toward becoming "good" with money.

It's a little like Anton Chekhov's gun. If there is a gun hanging on the wall in Act I of a play, then you can be sure it is going to be used by the end of the play. Money is also hidden in plain sight. You can be sure it is going to play a role in every act of your life.

These examples about money and your relationship to it just start a long list of what you can have if you let go of it.

Budget for Time Off as Well as Time On

If we want to get beyond bribing ourselves about money, tricking ourselves into understanding its reality, or wearing masks about money, we might take a good, long look at vacations. Vacating is emptying. It is not the time to buy as much stuff as we can or drink and eat as much as we can. It is a time to *de*habituate and *re*habituate.

Vacations are often to pretend to be a fisherman or that we live outside, under the stars, as more indigenous than the bloke who drives an hour a day to work in traffic.

If we get mastery over our budgets and our time (the objective of most sane people), we can take another kind of vacation, one at home, one of peace, one that doesn't fake how we live but lives and breathes tranquility into how we live. Less worry about missing our plane or packing our suitcase. More discovery of the holy spirits already in our midst. If we had more time regularly, we would need fewer hectic vacations. If we had more time regularly, we would also be masters of our work, then masters of our play. If we had more time regularly, most of us would have less money, and that would be thrilling.

One of the saddest things I hear is often in September: "I got back from my two weeks 'off' and Monday was great, but Tuesday I was exhausted again." Ah.

The real issue with vacations is the way we work too hard and too long most of the time. We might hope instead for a seamless step into September from August and into August from July.

As Eduardo Galeano argued, the human is half garbage and half marvel. We created systems that vacations pretend to console.

They are like capitalism and have grown too big for their britches. They make promises they don't keep. They have a well-advertised value not worth the price. They look more like virtue signaling than emptying. Many people have figured out that the real vacation is one they need at home, a habit of daily rest and weekly Sabbath keeping. Then, when the vacation comes, its expensive disappointment is less a surprise.

Sometimes I fear that vacations have become like Spirit airlines, a way to spend more and more on less and less. It often looked like Spirit was the cheapest airline in the sky. It is now bankrupt. Truthfully, it was always bankrupt, and it offered us something too good to be true. Or so we thought. Tickets for travel were sometimes as low as $48. But then comes the fine print. For a seat it is $16. For a water, $5. For use of the bathroom, another fee. (Just kidding.) For a checked bag, $35.

Once, early in the airplane crunch for space in the air, I got on another airline, United, and asked, after I sat down, where the rest of my seat was. The flight attendant had a good laugh. I had a terrible flight.

Vacations can be enjoyed anywhere. You can take the long walk home after work, if you are lucky enough to live close to your work and have not been put out of reach by small-c, late-stage capitalism and its tricks with your budget. To get an affordable house, you must drive longer. You can buy a bargain at a local hotel with a swimming pool for one day every month. You can feed the pigeons in your park. You can ride the bicycle path. You can get a massage once a month instead of once a year, if you don't book the whole resort but make your resort at home. You can do something that is *not* work every day, as a sign of Sabbath, especially if you have to work on Saturdays or Sundays. You can go to the opera on the radio on Saturday afternoon and serve margaritas to your friends and neighbors. Potluck suppers with friends can be almost as good as a really good restaurant. Time off is very inexpensive if you locate the low-cost forms of personal entertainment that abound.

Many of us get the feeling that we have vacated insufficiently or that we are a plant that has grown too large for its pot. If we do not find real soil to set our roots in soon, we will become awkward and sad, limbs reaching leadingly toward the sun at the window, wanting to feel the worms and wetness of early morning, but always kept outside of such experiences. We know we need to get away but we don't know how to do it, given the servitude we have donated to the system. That's the donation to cancel so we can make more fruitful ones instead.

Two weeks a year is a pittance. It is much less time off than we humans, at our marvelous best, need.

Ancient Testimonies about How to Use the Money We Have

Many scholars argue that the four gospels in the New Testament are one-half economic in nature. Wow. Here are a few examples.

1 John 3:16–18:

This is how we know what love is: Jesus Christ laid down his life for us. And we ought to lay down our lives for our brothers and sisters. If anyone has material possessions and sees a brother or sister in need but has no pity on them, how can the love of God be in that person? Dear children, let us not love with words or speech but with actions and in truth.

Acts 20:35:

In everything I did, I showed you that by this kind of hard work we must help the weak, remembering the words the Lord Jesus himself said: "It is more blessed to give than to receive."

Luke 11:13:

If you then, though you are evil, know how to give good gifts to your children, how much more will your Father in heaven give the Holy Spirit to those who ask him!

Matthew 6:19–21:

Do not store up for yourselves treasures on earth, where moths and vermin destroy, and where thieves break in and steal. But store up for yourselves treasures in heaven, where moths and vermin do not destroy, and where thieves do not break in and steal. For where your treasure is, there your heart will be also.

Malachi 3:10–12:

"Bring the whole tithe into the storehouse, that there may be food in my house. Test me in this," says the Lord Almighty, "and see if I will not throw open the floodgates of heaven and pour out so much blessing that there will not be room enough to store it.

I will prevent pests from devouring your crops, and the vines in your fields will not drop their fruit before it is ripe," says the Lord Almighty. "Then all the nations will call you blessed, for yours will be a delightful land," says the Lord Almighty.

In the world of folk wisdom, there is scripture and then there is common sense. One of my favorite folk wisdoms is from my father-in-law. Always give money if a relative or friend needs it but *never* call it a loan. Make it a gift. You are more likely to get it back.

Let's say a friend asks you if they can borrow $1 thousand to get them through the next couple of months, until their house sells. Or just need money and have no prospects to be paid back. Give it to them with gladness. Don't call it a loan. Call it a gift.

I loaned money to a woman in the Philippines once, because we had worked together on a great project. I knew she had to get her own place. She got it. I even know that she will pay me back some day. When I get the money, I am going to *re*loan it. Better to keep it in circulation than in my bank. Common sense says give money and make it a gift. If you are repaid, great. If not, then not. Reread each of these ancient wisdoms considering this little problem of loaning money to friends. See what you think. Life may be summed up as becoming your own testimony, ancient or innocent, either way.

12

Meditation and Prayer Prompts

You might want to use these prayers in a hundred-day process, learning how to pray regularly, but even more, to practice the slow presence of pause in your life.[1] Think of these days as a purchase of a spiritual spa. Price is zero.

One pause, prayer, or meditation per day for one hundred days might make you an expert on yourself and how you relate to money.

1. The Serenity Prayer, sometimes called the AA Prayer

Theologian Reinhold Niebuhr wrote the prayer in response to growing fascism in Europe. Since that writing, the prayer has been adopted by the highly influential and successful Alcoholics Anonymous (AA) movement. It has also been claimed by multiple people who think they wrote it. A good prayer works like this. We become so familiar with it that we think it is ours.

The prayer is all-purpose. It can easily be used to prompt our behavior and our thinking about our money.

Niebuhr's daughter, Elisabeth Sifton, wrote a book in 2003 about the prayer, and every page is worth reading if you want to know something about prayer. The title is *The Serenity Prayer*. Notably, Niebuhr wrote this prayer as he began to understand fascism in Europe.

Sifton insists that the most important language in the prayer are the words *can't* and *should*. Unfortunately, most of the thousands of revisions insert *can't* for *should* in the second stanza. Sifton's research proved to her that her father used the word *should*—as in "should be changed."

It is worth meditating on that matter alone when we think about money. Can it be changed or should it be changed or can't it be changed? Is it an addiction, an external force that has acquired too much power over us? Or is it something like harm reduction, where we reduce the harm our narratives place upon us? Can we reduce the harm money does to us and increase its positive gain?

Here I have called prayer alternatively: pause, meditation, action-reflection, or just reflection.

What follows are prompts for prayer or meditation about money.

The Serenity Prayer:

God, give us grace to accept with serenity the things that cannot be changed, courage to change the things that should be changed, and the wisdom to distinguish the one from the other.

The Lord's Prayer or "Our Father" better said as

Mother/Father God
Hallowed be Thy Name
Thy Kin dom Come
Thy will be done
On earth as it is in Heaven.

Give us this day our daily Bread.
Forgive us our debts,
As we forgive our debtors.
Lead us not into temptation
Deliver us from Evil
Because Thine is the Kin dom
And the Power and the Glory,
Forever and Ever,
Amen.

Padre/Madre Dios, Nuestro que estas en el Cielo
Santificado sea tu Nombre
Venga tu reino,
Hagase tu voluntad,
En la tierra como en el Cielo.
Danos Hoy Nuestro pan de cada dia
Perdona nuestras ofensas
Como Tambien nosotros perdonamos a los que nos ofenden.
No nos dejes caer en tentacion
Y ibranos del mal
Porque tuyo es el reino
Tuyo es el poder
Y tuya es la gloria, ahora y por siempre. Amen.

Read either of these prayers economically. Read them as economic behavior lessons.

The first one seeks the gift of wisdom about what we can and cannot do to live our best life.

The second one gives thanks for the reign of God, bringing heaven to earth.

2. Happy Workers at 4 a.m. on Sunday, January 15, 2025
(You could write a prayer any day, any time that told its story. That's how I did the prayer/poem that follows.)

> The attendant at the Omni was happy.
> She told me to add the address for the local airport.
> Uber drivers don't know we have an airport in New Haven.
> The Uber driver was happy.
> He knew where the open coffee shop was at 5 a.m.
> It opened at 4:30.
> Even on Sundays.
> Truck drivers go there.
> The coffee shop person was happy.
> She knew we'd want hot not cold that January morning.
> The moon was happy, setting but looking like it was rising.
> The airline attendant was happy.
> She didn't grumble about how long it took to figure out my ticket.
> The flight attendants were funny.
> They all wore boots.
> The man on the airport ground was happy.
> He walked us to our big airplane at the small airport.
> Tweed is its name.
> I flew Avelo for the first time.
> Avelo means Swift Bird.
> I was happy.

3. As the writer of this book, I pray with the reader, "Let this book be not yet another nuisance fee." Amen.

4. "It is more blessed to give than to receive" (Matthew 6:19–21). Is that really true? What if I feel like nobody gives me a damn thing? What if I am hungry for a gift? Can I get a gift if I give more, even when I am out of pocket?

5. What are the moths doing to me today?
"Do not store up for yourselves treasures on earth, where moths and vermin destroy, and where thieves break in and steal. But store up for yourselves treasures in heaven, where moths and vermin do not destroy, and where thieves do not break in and steal. For where your treasure is, there your heart will be also" (Matthew 9: 16–21).

6. What are the pests doing to my crops today?
"'Bring the whole tithe into the storehouse, that there may be food in my house. Test me in this,' says the Lord Almighty, 'and see if I will not throw open the floodgates of heaven and pour out so much blessing that there will not be room enough to store it. I will prevent pests from devouring your crops, and the vines in your fields will not drop their fruit before it is ripe,' says the Lord Almighty. 'Then all the nations will call you blessed, for yours will be a delightful land,' says the Lord Almighty" (Malachi 3:10–12).

7. Consider your children and grandchildren's ages in 2100.
What will life look like and be for them?

8. If we try to save what can be saved of our remaining earth, we will be met halfway by the divine, according to Bill McKibben. When did God meet me halfway? Or did God fail to show up so far?

9. Song of the chambermaid. She was changing the sheets on my bed as I left the hotel. I had forgotten something in the room. I interrupted her song. But it stuck with me. Now I always hum when I change my sheets at home too.

10. The season I love the most is the fall of the patriarchy. When will that season come? Or has it already come, and I didn't catch it? Why do men have so much more money than women?

11. The point of the human is to rise and to land. Am I rising or landing today? Which is more important?

12. What do people mean when they say, "You are the bee's knees" or "You are the cat's pajamas"? This old-fashioned language sounds like so much fun. It's also an alternative to cursing. Like saying "fooey" or "fiddle dee-dee" instead of "f——" or "damn" or "bull——." I wonder if I know how to bless and curse, be blessed and be cursed in interesting ways.

13. *Laudato Si'*. Why did the former pope write a book imitating Saint Francis and his love of animals and the earth? Why does the pope think the point of life is to praise God and love God forever? Where does that mandate show up on my to-do list today?

14. Did something bribe me or not?

15. Do I imagine that I own the sun? Do I need to go spiritually solar and let more of my energy come to me without my having to pay so much for it?

16. A Land Acknowledgment for Worship
    Leader: We are not the first peoples on this land.

People: Nor will we be the last.

Leader: We are not the best people ever here.

People: Nor are we the worst.

Leader: Grant us wisdom, grant us courage, for the facing of these days.

People: For the facing of these days. Amen.

Unison Prayer: When we reach for the power to understand our time and place, O God, grant us wisdom in doing so. Let us not compete with the past or the future but instead live our best here and now. Let us apply the Boy Scout method of leaving the place a little nicer than we found it. Let us be humble about our improvements and forgive us for the soil that has not been enriched by us. When we compare ourselves to others, stop us and let us find our own way in our own day. And let the Greta Generation lead us. Amen.

17. Do I have to go to church to sing hymns?
If not, today I will hum a little. Maybe:

God of Grace and God of Glory, Harry Emerson Fosdick Version
This Little Light of Mine, I'm Going to Let It Shine.
I've Got Peace Like a River in My Heart.

Do I have a theme song? Do I need one?

Some people wake up every day and sing, *"This is the day, this is the day, this is the day, that the Lord has made, let us rejoice, let us rejoice, let us rejoice and be glad in it and be glad in it."*

Old-timers never ate their food till they had given the "grace."

The prayer at table that gives thanks.

18. Perhaps when I do the recycling or the composting or take the garbage out, I can marvel at how much I have.

19. Merciful God, we seek in holy love to save all people from the aimlessness of sin, the sin of separation from you, the sin of being curved in on ourselves, the sin of not knowing our own glory, the sin of hurting ourselves and hurting others. Amen. (Old prayer, author unknown.)

20. Complex creator, you made us mostly of water and doused us with chemistry, the kind that often becomes our master. Assure us that we have free will even if we forget. Amen.

21. Creator of righteousness, renew our right relation with all that was, is, and will be.

22. Relieve us of shame and blame toward ourselves or each other and remind us of our original blessing and kick original sin out the door. Amen.

23. Universal God, you who neither specialize nor discriminate, remind us regularly that people who use drugs, and the people who love them, are first human and worthy of all the protections you bestow on us so that we may bestow them on each other. Amen.

24. Create in us a new heart and uphold a right spirit within us; cast us not away from your presence and take not your holy spirit from us. Amen. (Ancient prayer.)

25. Restore unto us the joy of your salvation and grant us your peace. (Ancient prayer.)

26. Reducer of harm, granter of renewal, you who wait close by no matter where we are or who we have become, help us to create strong movements of harm reduction in all walks of life, including the walk with addiction. Amen. (From the ordination paper of Erica Poellot [EP].)

27. Storied spirit, teach us the regular and habitual expression of radical welcome, the welcoming of all stories and paths, and help us call each other name and to cherish particularity. Make sure we have good friends who are both rich and poor. Amen. (EP paper.)

28. God of hospes, not hostes, grant us a constant hospitality that seeks people out, meets them where they are, and invites them into loving community. When we are tempted to blame people for their poverty or their addictions or their misery, show us to the mirror and there let us take a long look at ourselves. Amen.

29. Come as you are, no matter how broken, no matter how harmed, no matter how fragile, and find a sacred space where no one is refused. Amen. (EP paper.)

30. Burden-bearer, remind us of how hard people are working, creatively, desperately, intently, and faithfully, struggling to find ways to carry their burdens. Especially work with those who really work, from sun up to sun down, building highways and roads, forging the sea, flying the plane, taking care of the sick, the lame, the dispossessed. Amen. (EP paper.)

31. Open a vein and a room where people can tell their stories, be their stories, tell and be their whole stories and to show up with their whole selves. Amen. (EP paper.)

32. Awesome God, help us to stand at awe at a harm reduction that joins you in standing in awe at the burdens that people carry, rather than with judgment at how they get through. Amen. (EP paper.)

33. You of the embossed invitation, send us each the divine invitation to come, with all their you, weary and carrying heavy burdens and give us rest. Amen. (EP paper.)

34. I heard God say: Come just as you are. You are right, loved, and wholly enough. Holy and enough. Amen. (EP paper.)

35. Put a stone in my pocket, let me rub it from time to time, let it calm me. Let me give it away to my friend as a gesture of kindness. Amen.

36. Rehumanize those who have been dehumanized. Create subjects, out of objects. Make sure people who use drugs are people. Make sure people who are unemployed aren't embarrassed. Make sure college students enjoy their business courses and are also free to take art. Give everyone a name. Not a frame. Amen.

37. Drive me to figure out what blame and shame ever did for me. Amen.

38. Upton Sinclair came home from a few days away to find that uninvited picnickers had raided his kitchen, smoked his cigarettes, and gone swimming in his pool. "I don't think," he told *The New York Times*, "that they read any of my books." Let us have an odd response the next time we are robbed.

39. Help me to understand what it means to be personally invaded or robbed or to have hired a moving truck whose contents never arrived. Help me to understand what it is like if my house burns down. Amen.

40. So many people are at the end of their strength or luck. Flannery O'Connor wrote stories about people who were complete in their smallest gestures, or in a moment's involuntary action that could decide a life forever. Old Mr. Fortune, in "View of the Woods," loves his granddaughter so much that he kills her without meaning to. The young son of the dissolute city couple in "The River" is taken by his babysitter to see a country baptism, goes back by himself, and drowns trying to find his new friend Jesus in the river.
Help us renew our strength by knowing that we are not alone in weird experiences. Amen.

42. Alec Baldwin's story! How will that end? What a human text it is. The case against him is dismissed. People loved to hate him because they thought he was rich. I know him. The story of the murder will never end. Some things just stick.
How do we hate the rich better?

43. Mark Twain's remedy for a cold: "Plain gin was recommended, then gin and molasses, then gin and onions. I took all three." What if you are an alcoholic and can't stop drinking and have a cold? Or have no sense of humor? Or are "only" addicted to money, not the hard stuff?

44. How do you celebrate when you don't drink? Or go to a party or a wedding? How? How to give a gift when you can't afford it? Or be in a wedding party where you must buy dresses that cost thousands? How

do you show up at the party "just as I am, without one plea"? How much different do you want to be from other people?

45. What if it is true that everybody is equally marginal, including rich white people? They just don't know it yet.

46. Kwok Pui-Lan defines colonialism as thinking your colony is the greatest. Of course, you are wrong.

47. Treat your awakening words as though God was listening. Or just go ahead and go to sleep; God is the one who is awake and woke. Whatever happened to the word *woke*? How did it become so neglected and disrespected? Wasn't there a Great Awakening a couple of times in America?

48. We pray for all of those who have buckled under the stress ... including ourselves. Amen.

49. The new fifth stage of grief: Making meaning out of denial, anger, acceptance, bargaining. Making meaning out of being a loser, a failure, a ne'er do well. Making meaning out of money and the loss of it.

50. The new thinking about addiction and masks: they are a loss of narrative and a loss of transcendence. We can't get high naturally so we get high with substances that we purchase. If you have lost a through line to your narrative and making money has become it, you might also lose transcendence. That would be even more costly.

51. The new thinking about trauma: failed witness is what causes trauma. The failure to witness happens when nobody notices how much it hurts. Can you notice? Can you ask people to notice you?

52. The new thinking about healing: when somebody notices and says so out loud. Can you talk out loud?

53. "'I just want you to shut up,' God says, 'and let you know how much I love you.'" Says Brené Brown.

54. "Connection. Its opposite is shutting down or acting out." (Brené Brown)

55. "When a person makes a bid for connection, we often don't just stay vulnerable with the person. Usually, we scold or fix or instruct rather than listening with curiosity."[2] (Brené Brown)

56. Inspiration comes in many forms, and often in the form of the "Spirit's Nudge." Like a dog gives you when it knows you've lost the trail and nudges you back on it. Or a call just at the right time from the right person makes you wonder why you lost so much time worrying.

57. Have you ever had a really good garage sale or decluttering? What did it feel like?

58. "Why do you spend your money for that which is not bread, and your labor for that which does not satisfy?" (Isaiah 55:2)

59. What is the best gift you have ever given anyone? What is the worst? What is the best gift anyone ever gave you? Was it expensive? Or just thoughtful?

59. Charlotte Perkins Gilman wrote in *Women and Economics* (1898) that women were suffering under the weight of their own possessions; her life had become keeping her things clean.

60. Just how pagan are we? Don't we love solstice as much as Christmas and tents as much as houses? Maybe to have a good prayer we need to be outside.

61. Some people were not held by their mother or father. Imagine not being held by your mother—and looking for a cleft the rest of your life.

62. Great flow, even larger than great waters, dividing and reuniting, place us in that gymnastic zone, the judgment-free place, where our fat and our flaws matter less than our faith, our lollygagging and loneliness matter less than our love, and our own judgments and jealousies matter less than your justice.

63. Breathe on me Breath of God.
Holy Spirit, you who invoke so much shame in me, draw near and relieve me of my hammers, my nails, my thorns, my self-punishments. Breathe a new breath in me, let it be less dark, less in need of mouthwash, fresher and refreshing as a shower, more amusing than amazing. Let me stand strong on my own two feet—and let dependency be a story about my past. Let it become the foundation of my unconditional and nonjudgmental experience of others. Amen.

64. Don't use the word *should* on yourself or the beloved. *May* is a good substitute. "You may quit hurting yourself," not "you must quit hurting yourself."

65. Don't try to fix people. You are not a repair person. You are also in need of repair. Relationship is better than repair.

66. Just say "tell me more." And listen. Really listen. Don't spend your time thinking about what you will say or do next. Just "tell me more."

67. My music teacher told me, "What you put in the recorder is what you get out." Deposit in me the capacity to be thankful and make my music more beautiful day by day. When I forget a word of grace at table, tap me on the shoulder and give me another chance. Amen.

68. You might be thankful. You may be thankful. You could be thankful. You have the resources to be thankful. Give them a workout. Take the sticks and stones out of your bag … and build altars with the stones. Sit around a fire and warm yourself. God loves you. God wants beauty for you. Just beauty.

69. Do you do villain's monologues when you speak? Why? Does it help you to have someone to blame?

70. Familiar plot structures are at least "rags to riches" or "riches to rags." Or "the quest." Or "voyage and return." All stories have a beginning, a middle, and an end. When you talk to people, be a storyteller. Leave enough empty space for them to fill in the blanks. Most of us let money tell us its story. Instead, we need to tell the story of us and money our way, every day. It will also change over time. "It's all about the money" is a boring story.

71. Yes, we move at the speed of trust.

72. Progress is three steps forward and two steps backward. Sometimes it is three steps forward followed by three steps backward. Change is not easy. Change is hard.

73. If there is any room in the sky for prayers, let mine be heard in such a way that I help others pray and be heard.

74. The golden rule really matters: love your neighbor as you love yourself. Your neighbor is yourself. You are your neighbor. If you are not beloved, others will not be beloved either. If you are beloved, those who surround you will also be beloved. It is a circle.

76. Addiction, masking, not pausing to pray or think—reliance on external things—is often seen as narrative deficit disorder or the loss of a personal path. Why do some people get addicted and others don't? So many are lost and in appreciation deficit disorder mode. Why?

77. Spiritual care is care of the spirit—which is simultaneously care of the body. A sick body can be spiritually healthy, just like a well body can be spiritually unwell. Spirit for all seasons and during sickness and in health: How do we get to inner power, or the higher power, or the soul, or the meaning? How do we get that missing ingredient? Is it something we buy?

78. Care is different than fixing. It is mightily different than fixing. Care is engagement with the story as it is, not the story as you want it.

79. There is a big difference between powerless love and loveless power. How do we get to powerful love?

80. There is no perfect English counterpart for *mudita*, but the closest we can get to its definition is the idea of "sympathetic joy, unselfish joy, asking joy in the success of others," and to Buddhists, this is "pure joy, unadulterated by self-interest." This is not a temporary, transient,

cheerful state. This is a deep practice of embodying joy through solidarity with the joyful thriving of one another.

81. Less is more.

82. Regarding Dolly Parton and the Dalai Lama: "I'll tell you why I love her," said a Wisconsin housewife. "Dolly is everything I ever dared to be. Sure, she's outrageous looking. But just once, didn't you ever want to do something outlandish? Without worrying about what everyone will say? Plus, she always seems to be laughing, just like the Dalai Lama. I want to know why they are always laughing."
Maybe it is because neither has any malice toward anyone?

83. The perfect religious community does not exist. Finding a church is like finding a spouse. There are two dimensions: "Can I truly love this person, and will they love me?" But just as important: "Can I live with their imperfections (and can they live with mine)?"

84. Every human being will sooner or later let us down. Every spouse will be, in some way, a less-than-perfect life partner. So, part of the spiritual work of a good and healthy marriage is learning to love each other, in spite of both of your imperfections. Money is one of the largest subjects in any marriage. Good marriages are places where both people gain power over time. They may or may not gain money. But both gain power. And that power lets them create and recreate their money story. Richer/poorer; in sickness and in health; for better or for worse.

85. Imperfect people often get very rich. Less able or talented people sometimes don't. There is *not* a direct correlation between wealth and ability.

86. Let me go into my meetings today with a wiggle in my walk and a giggle in my talk. Spur me on to that great Day that is approaching. When I leave, let people compliment me on how much positive energy I and they now have. Amen.

87. This is what the Lord says—
> he who made a way through the sea,
> a path through the mighty waters ... (Isaiah 43:16)

What else can God do that we cannot?

88. Rehab is a wonderful thing. Rehab places are wonderful places. Restoring what is lost is a great virtue. Much better to prehab. Not to get weak in the first place. Pay attention to that. It may save you a lot of heartache, not to mention money.

89. Punishmentalists are people who love to criticize other people and lessen them. Stay away from them. Better yet, stop complaining, yourself. Make people more on your watch. Not less.

90. Calvin said the purpose of life is to love God and to praise God forever. You are to turn yourself into a tambourine of joy and praise. That joy and praise will accomplish all the secondary objectives, all by itself.

91. Nietzsche spoke of *amor fati*, an idea drawn from the Stoics, who taught that it was possible to transform the turns of Fortuna's wheel into virtues or art. There are conditions we cannot change; what we can have is a noble spirit. We can learn to love our fate.

We cannot insulate ourselves from suffering, but we can control the stories we build around it. This means a willingness to abandon the idea that life is a scorecard and to see it instead as a story.

92. Spiritual maturity is raising ourselves to full health so we can raise our children the same. We are the ones who need to be dropped off at Sunday School, not them.

93. Is it ever right to separate from a loved one because they keep getting fired or can't hold a job or help us support our household? No, it is never right. But it is sometimes more right to separate than to self-flagellate. Or to not admit that we are a part of the problem. Failure is not impossible. Failure is possible. Our own failure to love is also forgivable by God.

94. All people are fully worthy of love. All behaviors are not.

95. People can't stop talking about the church people in Charleston who prayed for the power to forgive their attacker. That generosity extends to our lives with money. If our children have no shoes, what are we to do? Sin is the refusal to be accountable, to manage our accounts. Sin is impotence, which we sometimes choose because we are so unaware of our own power.

96. Forgiveness is not a lofty spiritual goal so much as a practical way of being and living. It is efficient, cost effective, adaptive, and pragmatic. It is probably the most valuable thing in your entire bank account. And if it is not there, find it and put it there.

97. A good collection of one-sentence prayer cleans off the counter after the dishes are done. It collects your thoughts and makes them one. We wipe the counter down so that it sparkles while it's empty. Because our hearts and our counters are so rarely empty, this collecting and completion constitutes a spiritual moment.

98. Prayer is also listening and not just speaking. The clarification of the counter allows for something like quiet. It is a time of shutting up and not talking. It is a time of experiencing what we often forget to notice or acknowledge.

99. Incorporate aesthetic minimalism into the way you live. Even pray these one hundred prayers in that spirit. Make them beautiful to yourself. Add whimsy to them. "What if I." Or "Might I." Rewrite them for you. Read Duane Elgin's 1981 book, *Voluntary Simplicity*.

100. At my church, we open worship with the knowledge that we are not the first people on this land, nor will we be the last. We pray to God to give us help to be good ancestors.

My college at Gettysburg says it like this: "We live on the unceded and indigenous land, including the traditional homelands of the Susquehanna, the Conestoga, the Seneca, the Lenape, and the Shawnee nations. That same land is drenched in blood from the Civil War...."

Prayer is not just churchy. It is also simple acknowledgment. Or just a pause. Or creating a long memory, into which we put the experience of the day.

If praying these one hundred prayers, prompts, and meditations helped you for the last hundred days (or some approximation thereof), you could write your own prayers and collect them for the next hundred.

NOTES

Chapter 2

1. Borrowed with permission from Jamie Johnson, one of my students who wrote a paper on the subject for her Doctor of Ministry.
2. Viktor E. Frankl, *Man's Search for Meaning* (Beacon Press, 2006), 67.

Chapter 3

1. E. B. White and Katharine S. White, eds., *A Subtreasury of American Humor* (Capricorn, 1980). (Quoted multiple times here and includes the material on Arthur Frommer.)
2. Octavio Paz, "Use and Contemplation" (University of Bologna, 1973); posted July 4, 2020, at https://cordillerana.cl/en/blogs/hechoamano/el-uso-y-la-contemplacion-un-ensayo-de-octavio-paz

Chapter 4

1. The quote "Man's chief end is to glorify God, and to enjoy Him forever" comes from the *Westminster Shorter Catechism* (1647), not directly from John Calvin, though it reflects Calvinist theology and is often attributed to him.

   "Enjoying God" refers to finding ultimate fulfillment in relationship with God rather than in temporal things like having a good time or being promiscuous.

Chapter 5

1. Gus Wezerak, *The New York Times*, op-ed, May 7, 2024.
2. Rabbi Judith Shulevitz's material comes from a podcast interview with Ezra Klein, January 3, 2023 (https://www.nytimes.com/2023/01/03/podcasts/ezra-klein-show-transcript-judith-shulevitz.html), and her book *The Sabbath World: Glimpses of a Different Order of Time* (Random House, 2010).
3. T. S. Eliot, "Distracted from distraction by distraction" appears in his poem "Burnt Norton," which is the first of the *Four Quartets*, published in 1936.
4. Tony Cohan, *On Mexican Time: A New Life in San Miguel* (Broadway, 1999), 35.
5. The Trinity Red Bar quote is from an advertising brochure the restaurant uses.

Chapter 6

1. Social psychologist Hazel Henderson is known for whole-cost accounting and has written several books about it. Her books include *Creating Alternative Futures* (Kumarian Press, 1996, original edition, Berkley Books, 1978); *Ethical Markets: Growing the Green Economy* (Chelsea Green Publishing, 2006); and *Redefining Wealth and Progress: New Ways to Measure Economic, Social, and Environmental Change: The Caracas Report on Alternative Development Indicators* (Knowledge Systems Inc., 1990).

Chapter 8

1. Jim Rice, "The Virtue of Being Unhip," *Sojourners*, April 2024.

Chapter 10

1. "Writing on Chateau La Coste" previously published at www.chateau-lacoste.com/en/#

Chapter 12

1. The Pico Iyer quote about the urgency of slowing down is from his TED Talk, "The Art of Stillness," August 2014 (https://www.ted.com/talks/pico_iyer_the_art_of_stillness?language=en), and is also found in his book *The Art of Stillness: Adventures in Going Nowhere* (TED Books, 2014).

   In his TED Talk, Iyer stated: "In an age of acceleration, nothing can be more exhilarating than going slow. And in an age of distraction, nothing is so luxurious as paying attention. And in an age of constant movement, nothing is so urgent as sitting still."

2. Brené Brown, TED Talk, "The Power of Vulnerability," June 2010, https://www.ted.com/talks/brene_brown_the_power_of_vulnerability?language=en

ABOUT THE AUTHOR

Donna Schaper has been an ordained minister and activist for over fifty years. She has written thirty-nine books and hundreds of essays, features, and op-eds, including a humor series, "The Dolly Mama Does Religion." She has raised nearly $2 million over fifty plus years for not for profits and congregations. For the last two decades, she has written daily devotionals for the United Church of Christ website and is currently working as interim pastor at the United Church of Gainesville, Florida.